SECRETS TO BEING A RELEVANT SHEPHERD & MINISTER OF CHRIST

Amb Promise Ogbonna

CONTENTS

WHY I WROTE THIS BOOK!

I am sent to Publish All the Words of God's Heavenly Kingdom Life for the Restoration of all.

I am not writing human philosophy. I am not writing as a hobby neither am I writing to entertain but to bring Spiritual light, impart Spiritual Wisdom and Power to build your faith and transform your life! I have a Mandate from The Lord Jesus Christ to write and these Words are published to meet man's needs in every area of life! This Book, therefore, is published in obedience to the Command of the Lord to make His Words of Life and Wisdom Solutions and Power available to address every aspect of human needs.

I can say as Paul wrote "My message and my preaching were not in the persuasive language of philosophy, but in demonstration of the Spirit and of power; in order that your faith should rest, not on human philosophy, but on the power of God." 1Corinthians 2:4-5 (BBE)

"For the Kingdom of God is based, not on words, but on power." 1Corinthians 4:20 (BBE)

The Life Publishing Mandate

The Lord sent me to Publish All The Words of His Heavenly Kingdom Life for ALL mankind!

Jesus' last words is to Preach and Publish the Good news with proofs to every creature and among all nations (Mark 13:10; 16:15; Matthew 24:14).

The Lord gave us the Good news to publish and spread among all nations (Psalm 68:11; Mark 13:10).

In the Book of Esther, the enemy wrote and spread the words of death worldwide to destroy God's people and souls that God loves. [see Esther 3].

But at the command of the king, a new decree and words of life were written and spread to reach everyone (every creature) everywhere that the first words of death had reached. [see Esther 8].

This is our task. We have been given the New Covenant, Heavenly Kingdom, Words of Life to publish and spread to reach every creature everywhere worldwide. The Good news is that no one needs to die again! The old decree has been changed. Everyone can now live and enjoy peace and prosperity where each lives. That is why Ontop Mission Life Publishers Company. We are Publishing, Spreading and Bringing the Gospel of Christ and All the Words of life to every creature everywhere.

I will like to share some of the encounters with the Lord Jesus Christ that gave birth to The Life Publishing Mandate and why this Book and my other books:

1. On 21/5/95, Jesus Christ and I stood on the balcony of a great beautiful mansion in Heaven whose foundation I couldn't see (see Amos 9:6). He showed me Preachers, driven by selfishness and being used by the enemy, walking on people's heads and shoulders as their platform to preach. The people were hungry, thirsty, weeping, trampled upon and yet yearning for the TRUTH (see Amos 8:11-13). I saw My Lord shaking His head in disgust. He also brought to my view those in hell and I saw their agony and pain and what a sight it was! Afterward, as we beheld the abuse of His people, He pointed His right hand towards them and said to me, "See what is happening to the people I died for. "The Lord Jesus gave me A WELL USED COPY OF THE BIBLE and said to me "GO and tell them (The Preachers and The People) to Repent and Believe The Gospel Only and they will be Restored." I asked 'How will I do it? And He said to me, "BE SEPARATE! Go, I send YOU as My Ambassador and Witness with My Authority and Power: Publish The Word, Stop anything after their destruction, Raise, Build and Plant them as My Ambassadors. Let them know the truth. Teach All The TRUTH and Spread them as My Seed ALL over the earth and restore all things."

2. On 6/7/96, The Lord Jesus Christ came to me again and said, "It is well" and gave me a copy of THE BIBLE and said to me, "Take: This is My Staff of Office" – My Authority and Power. After The LORD gave me His Staff of Office [The Word], I saw something like a mist or cloud appear out of the Word and as I watched, a horse emerged from 'within the mist' and jumped about and stopped. The Lord told me The Word is creative and created the horse and is My Rod for working Miracles, Wonders and Signs. I am to Go with it to all, as Moses went with his ROD, and "Stop anything after man's destruction, Bring Healing, Liberty and Restoration to all; Raise, Build and Plant Christ's Ambassadors everywhere and Restore all things."

3. On 20/5/97, I was given a BIBLE and 2 BIROS by Arch. Benson A. Idahosa in a conference that took place in a place like a stadium. And he said to me, "Go and Proclaim and Publish The Everlasting Gospel of Jesus Christ worldwide and deliver the full benefits to all. This Gospel of The Kingdom must be preached in all the world for a witness unto all nations!

4. On 18/11/03, The Lord spoke to me again ON WRITING, and said to me "Write all the hidden mysteries I show you and I will ensure it gets to all the Nations Prophetic writings is what unveils, reveals, makes known the revelation of the mystery hidden for ages long past. The surest way of unveiling the Gospel and proclaim Jesus Christ the Lord is through prophetic writings as God commanded so that all nations will believe and obey God.

5. On 26/11/03, The Lord spoke to me saying, "Write what people can read and understand. It's most important. Your writing must be readable and understandable. Write in such a way that a primary school pupil can read and understand My Words. "The common people heard me gladly." Everyone must read and understand My Words that you write.

6. On 2/10/04, The Lord Jesus explained to me the vision of 21/5/95 where I Stood with Him on the Balcony of the Mansion in Heaven and He showed me Preachers using the shoulders and heads of people as their platform to preach. They were hungry, thirsty and trampled underfoot yet yearning for the reality. And The Lord commanded me to WRITE and publish His Words for the downtrodden and for all."

7. On 10/12/04, The Lord said to me "Write in a book all the Words that I have spoken to you" and He gave me Jeremiah 30:2.

8. On 04/04/05, The Lord said to me "Publish the Word and bring healing, liberty and restoration to all everywhere." See Psalm 68:11 and Psalm 107:20.

9. On 23/12/05, The Lord said to me:
Publish The Words
Publish The Works
Publish The Wonders
Make My Deeds Known
Let Everyone See My Glory Everywhere
10. On 01/03/13, The Holy Ghost said to me:
Publish the Works of Jesus Christ everywhere
Advertise the Doings of Jesus Christ the Lord.
Make known the Miracles of Jesus Christ the Lord.
Bind the Testimony of the Acts of the Lord Jesus Christ.
Be My Witness of all My Signs and Wonders everywhere.
Share Testimonies of All I AM Doing forever.

Go and Tell All everywhere of All My Miracles and Wonders and Signs and All I have Done and Commanded you.

The Lord said to me "All who believe that I sent you and receive you as My Ambassador and receive your Words as My Words will experience all the Father sent me to make available to humanity!"

Like Peter, I can tell you "We have not followed cunningly devised fables, when we made known unto you the power and coming of our Lord Jesus Christ, but were eyewitnesses of his majesty." 2Peter 1:16

Beloved, every Word written in this Book is from The Lord and are His Wisdom and Heaven's Solutions packaged and released to deal with your challenges, solve your problems and meet your needs.

Read with an open heart, Believe and Receive The Truth and Pick the Lessons and engage them.

I know you will experience The One who is The Author, Perfecter and Finisher of your faith and Who is The Real Author of this Book. He is Jesus Christ, The Son of The Living God. And He is the Same yesterday and today and forever!

"O LORD, how manifold are Your works! In wisdom You have made them all. The earth is full of Your possessions." Psalm 104:24

I guarantee you that you will never be the same again as you embrace God's Wisdom in This Book!

God Bless you.

Your Brother and His Steward for the benefit of all,

Ambassador Promise Ogbonna

THE HEAVENLY MANDATE & VISION

The Heavenly Mandate

To Preach The Everlasting Gospel to Everyone everywhere, Stop anything after man's destruction, Bring Healing, Liberty and Restoration to ALL; Raise, Build and Plant All as Christ's Ambassadors on His Living Mission everywhere and Restore all things!

The Heavenly Vision

To Restore All Things Everywhere at All Cost and By All Means! Acts 3:21

FIRST WORDS

J esus said "And He said to them, "I saw Satan fall like lightning from heaven."

God says "Woe to the inhabitants of the earth and the sea! For the devil has come down to you, having great wrath, because he knows that he has a short time."

The greatest need of the Lord and the Church is for RELEVANT shepherds!

After these things the Lord appointed other seventy also, and sent them two and two before his face into every city and place, whither he himself would come. Therefore, said he unto them, The harvest truly is great, but the laborers are few: pray ye therefore the Lord of the harvest, that he would send forth laborers into his harvest. Go your ways: behold, I send you forth as lambs among wolves. Carry neither purse, nor scrip, nor shoes: and salute no man by the way. And into whatsoever house ye enter, first say, Peace be to this house. And if the son of peace be there, your peace shall rest upon it: if not, it shall turn to you again. And in the same house remain, eating and drinking such things as they give: for the labourer is worthy of his hire. Go not from house to house. And into whatsoever city ye enter, and they receive you, eat such things as are set before you: And heal the sick that are therein, and say unto them, The kingdom of God is come nigh unto you.

"Then Jesus went about all the cities and villages, teaching in their synagogues, preaching the gospel of the kingdom, and healing every sickness and every disease among the people. But when He saw the multitudes, He was moved with compassion for them, because they were weary and scattered, like sheep having no shepherd. Then He said to His disciples, "The harvest truly is plentiful, but the laborers are few. "Therefore, pray the Lord of the harvest to send out laborers into His harvest."

The greatest need of the hour is for Shepherds and Ministers of Christ that will be able to confront and stop Satan and care for and meet the needs of the sheep and flock of Christ.

This Book is written to enlist competent Shepherds who will do the Will of the Master.

CHAPTER 1

RELEVANT AND IRRELEVANT SHEPHERDS

The greatest need of the Lord and the Church is for RELEVANT shepherds!

Who is a shepherd?

1. A shepherd is one that leads the flock or sheep. Psalm 80:1 Give ear, O Shepherd of Israel, thou that leads Joseph like a flock.

2. According to Numbers 27:17, **A shepherd is one "Which may go out before them, and which may go in before them, and which may lead them out, and which may bring them in;** that the congregation of the LORD be not as sheep which have no shepherd."

3. From Psalm 23:1 "The LORD is my shepherd; I shall not want" we see **a shepherd as one who cares for the sheep or flock until there is no want among them.**

4. According to Isaiah 40:11 **A shepherd shall feed his flock: he shall gather the lambs with his arm, and carry them in his bosom, and shall gently lead those that are with young.**

5. Isaiah 44:28 Shows that **a shepherd shall perform all the pleasure of the Lord**: even saying to Jerusalem, Thou shalt be built; and to the temple, Thy foundation shall be laid.

6, Isaiah 63:11 makes it clear **that a shepherd is one empowered by God with His Spirit and anointing to bring the flock or sheep up out of the sea or pits of destruction that swallow up**

others.

7. A shepherd gathers, defends and protects the sheep or flock from all evils and danger'

Eze 34:5 And they were scattered, because there is no shepherd: and they became meat to all the beasts of the field, when they were scattered. {because...: or, without a shepherd}

Eze 34:12 As a shepherd seeketh out his flock in the day that he is among his sheep that are scattered; so, will I seek out my sheep, and will deliver them out of all places where they have been scattered in the cloudy and dark day. {As...: Heb. According to the seeking}

8. A shepherd delivers the sheep from the beasts and devourers.

Am 3:12 Thus saith the LORD; As the shepherd taketh out of the mouth of the lion two legs, or a piece of an ear; so, shall the children of Israel be taken out that dwell in Samaria in the corner of a bed, and in Damascus in a couch. {taketh: Heb. delivereth} {in Damascus...: or, on the bed's feet}

9. A shepherd meets every need of the sheep or flock: strengthens the diseased and weak, heals the sick, recovers the lost, restores the scared and driven away, etc.

Eze 34:8 As I live, saith the Lord GOD, surely because my flock became a prey, and my flock became meat to every beast of the field, because there was no shepherd, neither did my shepherds search for my flock, but the shepherds fed themselves, and fed not my flock; {because...: or, without a shepherd}

Eze 34:23 And I will set up one shepherd over them, and he shall feed them, even my servant David; he shall feed them, and he shall be their shepherd.

Eze 37:24 And David my servant shall be king over them; and they all shall have one shepherd: they shall also walk in my judgments, and observe my statutes, and do them.

10. A shepherd separates the sheep from the goats.

Mt 25:32 And before him shall be gathered all nations: and he shall separate them one from another, as a shepherd divideth his sheep from the goats:

11. A shepherd lays down his life for the sheep or flock.

John 10:11 I am the good shepherd: the good shepherd giveth his life for the sheep.

John 10:12 But he that is a hireling, and not the shepherd, whose own the sheep are not, seeth the wolf coming, and leaves the sheep, and flees: and the wolf catches them, and scatters the sheep.

12. A shepherd is one who knows ALL the sheep or flock and must bring ALL the sheep into the fold at all costs and by all means.

John 10:14 I am the good shepherd, and know my sheep, and am known of mine.

John 10:16 And other sheep I have, which are not of this fold: them also I must bring, and they shall hear my voice; and there shall be one-fold, and one shepherd.

Hebrews 13:20 Now the God of peace, that brought again from the dead our Lord Jesus, that great shepherd of the sheep, through the blood of the everlasting covenant, {covenant: or, testament}

Notice how Jesus proved His worth as a good shepherd in contrast to the other shepherds.

"And Jesus went about all the cities and villages, teaching in their synagogues, and preaching the gospel of the kingdom, and healing every sickness and every disease among the people. But when he saw the multitudes, he was moved with compassion on them, because they fainted, and were scattered abroad, as sheep having no shepherd. {fainted...: or, were tired and lay down} Then saith he unto his disciples, the harvest truly is plenteous, but the laborers are few; Pray ye therefore the Lord of the harvest, that he will send forth laborers into his harvest." Matthew 9:35-38

"After these things the Lord appointed other seventy also, and sent them two and two before his face into every city and place, whither he himself would come. Therefore, said he unto them, the harvest truly is great, but the laborers are few: pray ye therefore the Lord of the harvest, that he would send forth laborers into his harvest. Go your ways: behold, I send you forth as lambs among wolves. Carry neither purse, nor scrip, nor shoes: and salute no man by the way. And into whatsoever house ye enter, first say, Peace be to this house. And if the son of peace be there, your peace shall rest upon it: if not, it shall turn to you again. And in the same house remain, eating and drinking such things as they give: for the labourer is worthy of his hire. Go not from house to house. And into whatsoever city ye enter, and they receive you, eat such things as are set before you: And heal the sick that are therein, and say unto them, the kingdom of God is come nigh unto you." Luke 10:1-9

In 1Kings 22:17 it is written "And he said, **I saw all Israel scattered upon the hills, as sheep that have not a shepherd: and the LORD said, these have no master:** let them return every man to his house in peace."

Notice also the reaction of The Lord Jesus in Matthew 9:36-38 "But when he saw the multitudes, he was moved with compassion on them, because they fainted, and were scattered abroad, as sheep having no shepherd." Then saith he unto his disciples, the harvest truly is plenteous, but the laborers are few; Pray ye therefore the Lord of the harvest, that he will send forth laborers into his harvest."

They had shepherds but were as sheep without a shepherd! (Staff Workers)

They had Apostles, prophets, evangelists, pastors and teachers but were as churches, ministries, students and groups and fellowships without Shepherds.

They were harassed and helpless. Stop their harassment; give all of them all the help they need.

They were harassed by the devil, by evil forces, by lack, poverty, by oppression, by wicked spirits, sickness, etc. Right in the presence of their shepherds, they were harassed. Their shepherds could not stop the enemy from harassing them. They were harassed and helpless. That means their shepherds could NOT render help unto their flock. Why? Because they didn't have what it takes to give help to their flock.

Governing Council and Trustee members are present yet management team members are harassed and helpless.

International and National Directors are there, yet management teams are harassed and helpless.

Management team members and Directors are there yet Areas are harassed and helpless.

Area Directors are there, yet Zones and Ministers serving there are harassed and helpless.

Local Ministers and Staff Workers are there, yet student leaders and officials are harassed and helpless.

Zonal officials are there, yet the sheep are harassed and helpless.

What is my relevance if as a shepherd or Pastor placed over the sheep, the sheep is harassed and yet helpless? Do they really need me? Would it not be better if I am not there so that they could look for a shepherd that can take care of them than for me to be there and they are harassed and helpless?

If I can't offer help to them in the face of their harassment, am I really qualified to be called their shepherd?

Note that the Lord's request to "pray that the Lord of the harvest will send laborers to his vineyard" clearly shows that some of the "shepherds" over them weren't sent by Him (The Lord). So, who sent them? Not the Lord. So, who? Maybe man, maybe themselves, maybe their religious rulers, maybe their church or organization, maybe their "spiritual fathers," maybe their uncles, maybe their relatives, maybe their tribes men who want them there so as to escape joblessness, maybe the economic hardship of the day, maybe their need or greed, maybe their belly or stomach, maybe the enemy of God who wants them to work from within to destroy the flock. But the truth is that the Lord of the harvest did not send them. So, He says "Pray them out!"

Notice the state of the sheep in spite of their shepherds: They were harassed and helpless right in the presence of their shepherds. So why allow such shepherds to remain? Pray for their replacement!

It is written "And Jesus went about all the cities and villages, teaching in their synagogues, and preaching the gospel of the kingdom, and healing every sickness and every disease among the people." Matthew 9:35.

1. Teaching because they were ignorant and without knowledge.

2. Preaching because they were under the domain of darkness in captivity and needed to be set free as captives. Luke 4:18.

3. Healing because they were diseased and sick. They lacked help and needed help yet couldn't get in spite of all the shepherds they had working in their midst. (All such shepherd must be replaced if they fail to return and come to Jesus for their equipping- Matthew 11:28-30.

We must return and learn of Him or else we will be replaced. There is an opportunity for all to return. Therefore, this meeting Matthew 11:28-30 and Mathew 9:36-38-shows that Jesus having seen the helplessness if the laboring shepherds beckoned unto them to come apart a while so as to be redirected, refocused, re-informed, and then be released to go and be relevant. Matthew 11:28-30; Acts 19:1-12.

Why the NEED for Shepherds?

Lets us read Ezekiel 34 to see why God sent the True Shepherd to His Sheep of the House of Israel.

Ezekiel 34

1 ¶ And the word of the LORD came to me, saying,

2 "Son of man, prophesy against the shepherds of Israel, prophesy and say to them, 'Thus says the Lord GOD to the shepherds: "Woe to the shepherds of Israel who feed themselves! Should not the shepherds feed the flocks?

3 "You eat the fat and clothe yourselves with the wool; you slaughter the fatlings, but you do not feed the flock.

4 "The weak you have not strengthened, nor have you healed those who were sick, nor bound up the broken, nor brought back what was driven away, nor sought what was lost; but with force and cruelty you have ruled them.

5 "So they were scattered because there was no shepherd; and they became food for all the beasts of the field when they were scattered.

6 "My sheep wandered through all the mountains, and on every

high hill; yes, my flock was scattered over the whole face of the earth, and no one was seeking or searching for them."

7 ¶ 'Therefore, you shepherds, hear the word of the LORD:

8 "as I live," says the Lord GOD, "surely because My flock became a prey, and My flock became food for every beast of the field, because there was no shepherd, nor did My shepherds search for My flock, but the shepherds fed themselves and did not feed My flock"

-

9 'therefore, O shepherds, hear the word of the LORD!

10 'Thus says the Lord GOD: "Behold, I am against the shepherds, and I will require My flock at their hand; I will cause them to cease feeding the sheep, and the shepherds shall feed themselves no more; for I will deliver My flock from their mouths, that they may no longer be food for them."

11 'For thus says the Lord GOD: "Indeed I Myself will search for My sheep and seek them out.

12 "As a shepherd seeks out his flock on the day he is among his scattered sheep, so will I seek out My sheep and deliver them from all the places where they were scattered on a cloudy and dark day.

13 "And I will bring them out from the peoples and gather them from the countries, and will bring them to their own land; I will feed them on the mountains of Israel, in the valleys and in all the inhabited places of the country.

14 "I will feed them in good pasture, and their fold shall be on the high mountains of Israel. There they shall lie down in a good fold and feed in rich pasture on the mountains of Israel.

15 "I will feed My flock, and I will make them lie down," says the Lord GOD.

16 "I will seek what was lost and bring back what was driven away, bind up the broken and strengthen what was sick; but I will destroy the fat and the strong, and feed them in judgment."

17 ¶ 'And as for you, O My flock, thus says the Lord GOD: "Behold, I shall judge between sheep and sheep, between rams and goats.

18 "Is it too little for you to have eaten up the good pasture, that you must tread down with your feet the residue of your pas-

ture-and to have drunk of the clear waters, that you must foul the residue with your feet?

19 "And as for My flock, they eat what you have trampled with your feet, and they drink what you have fouled with your feet."

20 'Therefore thus says the Lord GOD to them: "Behold, I Myself will judge between the fat and the lean sheep.

21 "Because you have pushed with side and shoulder, butted all the weak ones with your horns, and scattered them abroad,

22 "therefore I will save My flock, and they shall no longer be a prey; and I will judge between sheep and sheep.

23 "I will establish one shepherd over them, and he shall feed them-My servant David. He shall feed them and be their shepherd.

24 "And I, the LORD, will be their God, and My servant David a prince among them; I, the LORD, have spoken.

25 "I will make a covenant of peace with them, and cause wild beasts to cease from the land; and they will dwell safely in the wilderness and sleep in the woods.

26 "I will make them and the places all around My hill a blessing; and I will cause showers to come down in their season; there shall be showers of blessing.

27 "Then the trees of the field shall yield their fruit, and the earth shall yield her increase. They shall be safe in their land; and they shall know that I am the LORD, when I have broken the bands of their yoke and delivered them from the hand of those who enslaved them.

28 "And they shall no longer be a prey for the nations, nor shall beasts of the land devour them; but they shall dwell safely, and no one shall make them afraid.

29 "I will raise up for them a garden of renown, and they shall no longer be consumed with hunger in the land, nor bear the shame of the Gentiles anymore.

30 "Thus they shall know that I, the LORD their God, am with them, and they, the house of Israel, are My people," says the Lord GOD.'"

31 "You are My flock, the flock of My pasture; you are men, and I am your God," says the Lord GOD.

In Matthew 15:26 and Matthew 10:6, we discover that God sent Jesus to lost sheep of the house of Israel and Jesus sent His disciples to the same lost sheep of the house of Israel.

Matthew 15:24 "But He answered and said, "I was not sent except to the lost sheep of the house of Israel."

Matthew 10:6 **"But go rather to the lost sheep of the house of Israel.**

Notice the seven conditions of the Sheep the necessitated the Need of the Shepherd:

1. Diseased or weak. Ezekiel 34:4
2. Sick. Ezekiel 34:4
3. Broken down and brokenhearted or shattered. Ezekiel 34:4
4. Driven away. Ezekiel 34:4
5. Lost or captured or captives. Ezekiel 34:4
6. Prey. Ezekiel 34:8; Isaiah 42:22
7. Spoils or meat. Ezekiel 34:8: Isaiah 42:22; Amos 3:12

It is important for me to state here that these seven (7-fold) state of the Sheep or flock are the reasons for the appointment of shepherds.

Every God appointed and sent shepherd is sent to address those 7-fold reasons can claim to have been appointed or is appointed by the Lord.

The harvest Jesus spoke about in John 4:34-38, Luke 10:2 and Matthew 9:36-38 is the same as the one The Lord God Almighty sent Jesus The True Shepherd to take care of.

Notice what Jesus did and what He sent His disciples to do:
Notice what Jesus did in Matthew 9:35-38

35 ¶ Then Jesus went about all the cities and villages, teaching in their synagogues, preaching the gospel of the kingdom, and healing every sickness and every disease among the people.

36 But when He saw the multitudes, He was moved with compassion for them, because they were weary and scattered, like sheep having no shepherd.

37 Then He said to His disciples, "The harvest truly is plentiful, but the laborers are few.

38 "Therefore pray the Lord of the harvest to send out laborers

into His harvest."

Notice what Jesus sent His disciples to do in Matthew 10:1-8

And when He had called His twelve disciples to Him, He gave them power over unclean spirits, to **cast them out, and to heal all kinds of sickness and all kinds of disease.**

2 Now the names of the twelve apostles are these: first, Simon, who is called Peter, and Andrew his brother; James the son of Zebedee, and John his brother;

3 Philip and Bartholomew; Thomas and Matthew the tax collector; James the son of Alphaeus, and Lebbaeus, whose surname was Thaddaeus;

4 Simon the Canaanite, and Judas Iscariot, who also betrayed Him.

5 ¶ These twelve Jesus sent out and commanded them, saying: "Do not go into the way of the Gentiles, and do not enter a city of the Samaritans.

6 "But go rather to the lost sheep of the house of Israel.

7 "And as you go, preach, saying, 'The kingdom of heaven is at hand.'

8 "**Heal the sick, cleanse the lepers, raise the dead, cast out demons. Freely you have received, freely give.**

Notice what the Lord says to the shepherds in Ezekiel 34:7-16 "7 ¶ 'Therefore, you shepherds, hear the word of the LORD: "as I live," says the Lord GOD, "**surely because My flock became a prey, and My flock became food for every beast of the field, because there was no shepherd, nor did My shepherds search for My flock, but the shepherds fed themselves and did not feed My flock**" -'therefore, O shepherds, hear the word of the LORD! 'Thus says the Lord GOD: "**Behold, I am against the shepherds, and I will require My flock at their hand; I will cause them to cease feeding the sheep, and the shepherds shall feed themselves no more; for I will deliver My flock from their mouths, that they may no longer be food for them.**" 'For thus says the Lord GOD: "**Indeed I Myself will search for My sheep and seek them out. "As a shepherd seeks out his flock on the day he is among his scattered sheep, so will I seek out My sheep and deliver them from all the places where**

they were scattered on a cloudy and dark day. "And I will bring them out from the peoples and gather them from the countries, and will bring them to their own land; I will feed them on the mountains of Israel, in the valleys and in all the inhabited places of the country. "I will feed them in good pasture, and their fold shall be on the high mountains of Israel. There they shall lie down in a good fold and feed in rich pasture on the mountains of Israel. "I will feed My flock, and I will make them lie down," says the Lord GOD. "**I will seek what was lost and bring back what was driven away, bind up the broken and strengthen what was sick;** but I will destroy the fat and the strong, and feed them in judgment."

No shepherd is appointed to shepherd himself but the sheep.

The chief and only task of the shepherd is to care for the sheep and ensure the sheep lacks nothing and is not in want of anything. Notice Jeremiah 23:1-4 and Psalm 23:1-6

Jeremiah 23:1-4 "Woe to the shepherds who destroy and scatter the sheep of My pasture!" says the LORD.

2 Therefore thus says the LORD God of Israel against the shepherds who feed My people: "You have scattered My flock, driven them away, and not attended to them. Behold, I will attend to you for the evil of your doings," says the LORD.

3 "But I will gather the remnant of My flock out of all countries where I have driven them, and bring them back to their folds; and they shall be fruitful and increase.

4 **"I will set up shepherds over them who will feed them; and they shall fear no more, nor be dismayed, nor shall they be lacking," says the LORD.**

Psalm 23:1-6

The LORD is my shepherd; I shall not want.

2 He makes me to lie down in green pastures; He leads me beside the still waters.

3 He restores my soul; He leads me in the paths of righteousness For His name's sake.

4 Yea, though I walk through the valley of the shadow of death, I will fear no evil; For You are with me; Your rod and Your staff, they comfort me.

5 You prepare a table before me in the presence of my enemies; You anoint my head with oil; My cup runs over.

6 Surely goodness and mercy shall follow me All the days of my life; And I will dwell in the house of the LORD Forever.

The assignment of every true shepherd is to ensure that the sheep is never in want of anything.

In Christ's Ambassadors Living Mission International, Jesus Mission Headquarters our assignment as His appointed and sent Ambassadors and Shepherds is to ensure that there is no want among all His flock.

Therefore, having come to this fountain of transfiguration for a transformation and translation into the kingdom of his dear Son, with all authority to reign, I see nothing that will stop you from returning as a ruler in Christ's own very class in Jesus Name.

AS His Shepherds, we must minister to the needs of the people and ensure the same reason Our Loving Father sent Jesus to accomplish is accomplished by us.

Remember the seven conditions of the Sheep the necessitated the Need for Shepherds:

1. The sheep are Diseased or weak and need to be strengthened. Ezekiel 34:4

2. The sheep are Sick and need to be healed. Ezekiel 34:4

3. The Broken down and brokenhearted or shattered need to be bound up. Ezekiel 34:4

4. The Driven away need to be brought back to the fold and secured. Ezekiel 34:4

5. The Lost or captured or captives need to be sought for, recovered and taken care of. Ezekiel 34:4

6. The Prey need to be delivered and rescued and recovered. Ezekiel 34:8; Isaiah 42:22

7. The Spoils or meat need to released and restored and preserved. Ezekiel 34:8: Isaiah 42:22; Amos 3:12

I want to state categorically here that these seven (7-fold) state of the Sheep or flock are the reasons for the appointment of every shepherd or minister of the Gospel and if you are not performing these tasks you are not appointed nor sent by The Lord of the harvest.

If that is the group you fall into you must do two things immediately:

1. Leave the Lord's sheep peacefully, quietly and immediately in your own interest.

2. Come to Christ's Ambassadors Living Mission International, Jesus Mission Headquarters or get in touch with us as soon as possible. Matthew 11:28-30

Every God appointed and sent shepherd is sent to address those 7-fold problems.

CHAPTER 2

*THE FEAR OF DEATH IS MAN'S
MAJOR PROBLEM BUT JESUS
CHRIST HAS DEALT WITH THAT*

Hebrews 2:14 "Forasmuch then as the children are partakers of flesh and blood, he also himself likewise took part of the same; that through death he might destroy him that had the power of death, that is, the devil;"

Because of fear of death, man has lived subject to a lifelong bondage.

Because of fear of death-through lack, wants and poverty-man has lived subject to a life-long bondage in servitude seeking for food.

Because of fear of death-through sickness/disease-man has lived subject to a life-long bondage in the hands of physicians, doctors of no value who the enemy has used to rob them, kill and destroy them.

Because of fear of death, man has surrendered himself to untold suffering and hardship which God never meant for man.

But Jesus partook of the same nature as we do and came and died so as to destroy (and did destroy) (-cf Colossians 2:13-15; Hebrews 2:14-15) him who has the power of death, that is the devil. (Jesus through his death destroyed the devil who has the power of death) and hath delivered all who through fear of death were <u>SUBJECT</u> to lifelong bondage.

Note: The devil had the power of death. That means, whatever had the potency to kill was in Satan's control. So, Satan is behind poverty, disease/sickness, he is behind all forms of fear plaguing mankind. Satan is behind all kinds of oppression (John 8:44; 10:10; Acts 10:38). He is behind death (John 10:10; Hebrews 2:14; John 8:44).

1Corinthians 15:24-26- All the things that the enemy used to keep man subject to a lifelong bondage have been destroyed by Jesus. (See 1Corinthians 15:54-57).

Man's problem-which has kept him subject to a lifelong bondage till the present is "the fear of death"-through lack, sickness, poverty, demonic/evil charms, etc.

The reason why young people are doing all kinds of evil works is because they don't want to die. The fear of death-through failure in school has caused many to do what they are ashamed of.

The fear of death (through starvation, etc) has made people that are called, equipped and anointed and sent to a place to serve the Lord run away. We are not eager to lose our lives. We want to save it because of the fear of death and so have gotten involved in what we are not supposed to be involved in.

If the fear of death is dealt with, believers will be and live free. Jesus hath dealt/destroyed the devil. We are now free and must live free. Know this truth and live.

John 8:32, 36

32 "And ye shall know the truth, and the truth shall make you free.

36 If the Son therefore shall make you free, ye shall be free indeed."

The fear of death is man's major problem. But Jesus Christ has dealt with that by destroying the devil himself who hath the power of death and has used that power to cause many untimely deaths.

Always Remember: That the devil hath the power of death.

But it is written:

"Behold I (Jesus) give you power (Authority/power) to tread on serpent (the devil, Satan, Dragon) and scorpions (-all the evils the enemy uses to attack you) and over all the power of the enemy (even the power of death) and nothing shall by any means hurt you/harm you.

Jesus couldn't have said so if he has not completely and totally destroyed/disarmed the enemy (Hebrews 2:14; Colossians 2:14-15).

By the power Jesus gave to us, the fear of death is under our control. That means, we have all it takes to deal with all the forces that the evil and wicked one uses to cause man's death.

That means in reality that no weapon formed against us can stand (Isaiah 54:15-17).

That means we have been delivered- Hebrews 2:15; Colossians 1:13; and so, we must show it.

This shows we can take any right step towards the fulfillment of life's purposes not being afraid that the Lord will fail to take care of us.

That means we can go to wherever the Lord sends us not mindful of the "challenges" our minds may show us.

That means, we can go being willing to lay down our lives, not being afraid of death because we know we cannot die but must find our lives –Luke 9:24.

The "fear of death" has been conquered. All we need do now is to begin to "live by faith" for the justified shall live by faith to please God and attract his presence and provisions (Hebrews 2:4; Romans 1:17; Galatians 3:11; Hebrews 10:38; Hebrews 11:6).

Never allow the fear of death keep you subject to lifelong bondage. Be free and live. Live/walk by faith. For with faith, you stop all the fiery darts of the enemy's arrows. (Ephesians 6:16).

May your faith fail not. (Luke 22:31).

Keep your faith. (Luke 18:8).

Live by faith. (Habakkuk 2:4).

Walk by faith. (2Corinthians 5:7).

Do all things by faith. (Romans 14:23).

If we can do away with the "fear of death" by faith, then nothing shall be impossible unto us in Christ Jesus.

The reason why mankind is still living subject to a lifelong bondage, slavery/enslavement is because of the fear of death. If the fear of death could be dealt with, mankind will be free and live free.

Almost every step man takes in life is founded on his being afraid to die. No one wants to die. Almost everyone is afraid of death. And because men are afraid of death, they go into doing what they ordinarily shouldn't do.

That means, if man could be helped to understand that the things, he is afraid of as having the power to kill him are not there (because someone has dealt with them), they will become free and live to enjoy their life time on earth.

"Subject to lifelong bondage" is Satan's wish but the Lord's works have been done to enable man enjoy a lifetime/lifelong freedom and liberty. Only FAITH in all Jesus hath done can place this kind of life into man's hands. Why not believe in Jesus Christ today and live? (1John 3:23).

The reason why people don't give so as to prosper is because of the fear of death after giving. The reason why people can't believe God to heal them and their wards is because of fear of death. The reason why so many cannot leave their jobs to go and serve the Lord in foreign lands is because of the fear of death. The reason why God's own people do not love others practically and demonstrational is because of the fear of death. The reason why it is difficult for "believers" to lay down their lives today for the Master is because of fear of death.

The reason why so many believers are working in places (doing jobs they don't like in companies they know are satanic) is because of the fear of death. Almost everything that mankind engages and indulges in today is founded basically because of his fear of death.

The enemy knows it and uses the power of death as his tool to keep mankind tied down subject to lifelong bondage because of the fear of death.

Until you are delivered from the power/fear of death, you are still living subject to lifelong bondage. You are not yet free. You are bound. You are living under the domain of the devil. You must be set/made free. That's why Jesus came that's why He sent me to you.

1. Hebrews 2:14

"Forasmuch then as the children are partakers of flesh and blood, he also himself likewise took part of the same; that through death he might destroy him that had the power of death, that is, the devil;"

Jesus came to destroy the devil himself. And he has done that.

2. 1John 3:8

"He that committeth sin is of the devil; for the devil sinneth from the beginning. For this purpose, the Son of God was manifested, that he might destroy the works of the devil."

Jesus came to destroy all the works of the devil. And he has done that.

And now that both the devil and all his works have been destroyed, why must you live on in bondage all your lifetime.

The truth liberates. I am here to show you the truth so that you can live.

Both the devil and his works have been destroyed.

1. Hebrews 2:14

"Forasmuch then as the children are partakers of flesh and blood, he also himself likewise took part of the same; that through death he might destroy him that had the power of death, that is, the devil;"

The devil is destroyed.

2. 1John 3:8

"He that committeth sin is of the devil; for the devil sinneth from the beginning. For this purpose, the Son of God was manifested, that he might destroy the works of the devil."

His works are destroyed.

Why believe in lies and live your life in lifelong bondage? This is your hour of freedom and liberation. Nothing will keep you down anymore.

Do not fear him (the devil-with the power of death) who can only kill the body but fear God who will both kill the body and destroy the soul in hell fire. (Luke 12:4-7). Only God is to be feared. Not the devil. Never!

Proverbs 29:25-The fear of man bringeth snare. But the fear of the Lord liberates from all holds.

Psalms 23:4 I fear no evil because I fear no devil.

When you fear any evil, it is an expression of the fact that you fear the devil who can do evil. But when you do not fear the devil, you are not afraid of any evil.

I fear no evil because the Lord is with me (Psalms 23:4; Mark 16:20; Matthew 28:20; Hebrews 13:6; Romans 8:31).

No hair on my head can fall to the ground unless my father wishes/wants it to. So, what can the devil do? Nothing!

CHAPTER 3

*AMBASSADORS TO EXPECT
GREAT AND MIGHTY MIRACLES
EVERYDAY AND ALWAYS*

Luke 10:1-15

1 After these things the Lord appointed other seventy also, and sent them two and two before his face into every city and place, whither he himself would come.

2 Therefore said he unto them, the harvest truly is great, but the labourers are few: pray ye therefore the Lord of the harvest, that he would send forth labourers into his harvest.

3 Go your ways: behold, I send you forth as lambs among wolves.

4 Carry neither purse, nor scrip, nor shoes: and salute no man by the way.

5 And into whatsoever house ye enter, first say, Peace be to this house.

6 And if the son of peace be there, your peace shall rest upon it: if not, it shall turn to you again.

7 And in the same house remain, eating and drinking such things as they give: for the labourer is worthy of his hire. Go not from house to house.

8 And into whatsoever city ye enter, and they receive you, eat such things as are set before you:

9 And heal the sick that are therein, and say unto them, the kingdom of God is come nigh unto you.

10 But into whatsoever city ye enter, and they receive you not, go your ways out into the streets of the same, and say,

11 Even the very dust of your city, which cleaveth on us, we do wipe off against you: notwithstanding be ye sure of this, that the kingdom of God is come nigh unto you.

12 But I say unto you, that it shall be more tolerable in that day for Sodom, than for that city.

13 Woe unto thee, Chorazin! woe unto thee, Bethsaida! for if the mighty works had been done in Tyre and Sidon, which have been done in you, they had a great while ago repented, sitting in sackcloth and ashes.

14 But it shall be more tolerable for Tyre and Sidon at the judgment, than for you.

15 And thou, Capernaum, which art exalted to heaven, shalt be thrust down to hell."

Everywhere Jesus went He did great and awesome deeds. We are to follow His example daily.

Matthew 11:1-6

1 ¶ And it came about that when Jesus had come to the end of giving these orders to his twelve disciples, he went away from there, teaching and preaching in their towns.

2 Now when John had news in prison of the works of the Christ, he sent his disciples

3 To say to him, are you he who is to come, or are we waiting for another?

4 And Jesus, answering, said to them, Go and give news to John of the things which you are seeing and hearing:

5 The blind sees; those who were not able to, are walking; lepers are made clean; those who were without hearing, now have their ears open; the dead come to life again, and the poor have the good news given to them.

6 And a blessing will be on him who has no doubts about me.

As His Ambassadors, we are to open the way for the Lord to reach, heal, deliver and bless the people.

"Then He called His twelve disciples together and gave them power and authority over all demons, and to cure diseases. He sent them to preach the kingdom of God and to heal the sick. And He said to them, "Take nothing for the journey, neither staffs nor bag nor bread nor money; and do not have two tunics apiece. "Whatever house you enter, stay there, and from there depart. "And whoever will not receive you, when you go out of that city, shake off the very dust from your feet as a testimony against them." So, they departed and went through the towns, preaching the gospel and healing everywhere." Luke 9:1-6

"After these things the Lord appointed seventy others also, and sent them two by two before His face into every city and place where He Himself was about to go. Then He said to them, "The harvest truly is great, but the laborers are few; therefore, pray the Lord of the harvest to send out laborers into His harvest. "Go your way; behold, I send you out as lambs among wolves. "Carry neither money bag, knapsack, nor sandals; and greet no one along the road. "But whatever house you enter, first say, 'Peace to this house.' "And if a son of peace is there, your peace will rest on it; if not, it will return to you. "And remain in the same house, eating and drinking such things as they give, for the laborer is worthy of his wages. Do not go from house to house. "Whatever city you enter, and they receive you, eat such things as are set before you. "And heal the sick there, and say to them, 'The kingdom of God has come near to you.' "He who hears you hears Me, he who rejects you rejects Me, and he who rejects Me rejects Him who sent Me." Then the seventy returned with joy, saying, "Lord, even the demons are subject to us in Your name." Luke 10:1-9,16-17

We are to open the way for the LORD to come in into All places where He has not been to.

John introduced Jesus-Matthew 3:3; Luke 3:1-4; Isaiah 40:3-4.

John was a voice. An original. He was not an ECHO!

Jesus was a voice-John 5:19-20; 12:48-50; 14:31.

The Lord said to me "Always tell all the people to expect a miracle and to expect a new miracle every day. We must expect great miracles every day."

We must expect great, mighty and many miracles everyday.

See Matthew 27:50-54. It is written "And Jesus cried out again with a loud voice, and yielded up His spirit. Then, behold, the veil of the temple was torn in two from top to bottom; and the earth quaked, and the rocks were split, and the graves were opened; and many bodies of the saints who had fallen asleep were raised; and coming out of the graves after His resurrection, they went into the holy city and appeared to many. So, when the centurion and those with him, who were guarding Jesus, saw the earthquake and the things that had happened, they feared greatly, saying, "Truly this was the Son of God!"

At Jesus death, see what happened-

1.The veil of the temple tore from the top down.

2.The earth did quake and was opened.

3.The Rocks rents and split open.

4.The graves were opened.

5.Many bodies of dead saints arose and came back to life each with a brand-new body [flesh and bones].

6.The dead saints came out of their graves when Jesus resurrected and came out of the grave.

7.The risen saints went into the holy city and showed themselves to many.

8.The centurion and the army officers feared greatly and began to testify that "Truly, Jesus is the Son of God"

Note: Just as Jesus left the grave clothes and came out clothed (not naked), even so did all the saints that arose came out clothed.

Note: Ezekiel prophesied before the dry bones came together, were covered with flesh and stood up a mighty army.

But after Jesus' death and resurrection, nobody prophesied to the bodies of the dead saints, but the Mighty Restoring Power of God displayed put back flesh, eyes, nose, liver, pancreas, testes, uterus, toes, nails, hairs, even clothing upon them all and they came with the same faces and features they had such that all their people to whom they appeared recognized them.

Whatever you need to appear your normal best self, I command that restored back to you.

Males and Females had all they needed in their bodies before they made appearances to their own people.

Nothing about them was missing (Job 5:24).

They were whole, intact, the same.

I expect miracles beyond this in my lifetime as I go about with His Assignment for my life-to Heal all. Jesus said to me "Teach and preach and Heal all- no matter their sickness or disease."

The death and resurrection of Jesus was to enforce restoration of man's physical features. The spirit was with God. The bones were in the grave. But the death and resurrection of Jesus enforced the restoration of their physical bodies and souls and they arose and came out of their graves.

Jesus' death and Resurrection was to Enforce Man's Healing-Primarily

At His Resurrection, dead, decayed, buried bodies of Saints were Restored to life, with sound bodies and they came out of the grave and made appearances to many who recognized them.

When Jesus came back to life, they came back also.

When He arose, they also arose.

He came out with a clean healthy flesh and body.

They equally did.

His death and resurrection are to enforce the Healing of all that believe and receive.

2Timothy 1:10- Jesus hath abolished death and brought life and immortality to light through the gospel.

Romans 1:16 Preach the gospel of the kingdom and open the way for the healing of all caged presently.

Matthew 27:50; John 19:30-Jesus CRIED- IT IS FINISHED.

It is finished. Sin, Satan, sickness, slavery and all other evils must be stopped at all cost and by all means.

CHAPTER 4

STOP ALL SICKNESSES AND DISEASES IN THEIR BODIES AND DEATH IN THEIR SPIRITS

It is written in 1 Corinthians 6:20- You have been bought with a price. Glorify God in your body and spirit which are His.

1Corinthians 7:23- You have been bought with a price. Do not be slaves/servants of men (but servants of God).

1Peter 1:18-19-Leave the worthless way of our fathers which have been handed down to us. (cf Galatians 5:1).

2Corinthians 4:10-11- Let the life of Jesus be made manifest in our mortal bodies.

Remember John 6:63- The Living Word= Spirit and life/health to all our flesh (Proverbs 4:22).

2Timothy 1:10- Jesus (The Living Word made flesh, John 1:14/ Deity in bodily form) hath abolished death (all that destroys man's body and physical death and spiritual death) and hath brought life (health/healing-Proverbs 13:17; 4:22; John 6:63; John 10:10) and immortality to light by the gospel.

Galatians 5:11- Stand free in His liberty having been made free from the worthless, unprofitable, futile ways handed down to us.

Sickness, disease, poverty, lack and want, evils, slavery etc do not glorify God. Physical confinement nor spiritual slavery never brings Him glory.

John 10:10 shows that the devil comes only to steal and to kill and to destroy.

But because of the Lord's presence, none of the works of the enemy is to touch you because none of them ever gives Him glory. Why then must we go through them? Failure, defeat, and all the evil works of Satan are bad news and do not glorify the Lord Jesus Christ.

We must not spread such bad and sad news henceforth.

Our assignment is to preach THE EVERLASTING GOODNEWS!

The worst people will be saved and filled with The Holy Spirit.

The most terrific Catholics, Moslems, Orthodox and very religious folks will be saved and filled with the Holy Spirit.

The most dangerous gangsters will be saved and delivered and filled with The Holy Spirit.

The hardest rogues, criminals and fraudsters will be saved, delivered and filled with the Holy Spirit.

The most rebellious scoffers, scorners, mockers and slanderers will be saved, delivered and filled with The Holy Spirit.

This is what Relevant Shepherds are sent to accomplish.

Acts 2:17-22 says

16 "But this is what was spoken by the prophet Joel:

17 'And it shall come to pass in the last days, says God, That I will pour out of My Spirit on all flesh; Your sons and your daughters shall prophesy, your young men shall see visions, your old men shall dream dreams.

18 And on My menservants and on My maidservants, I will pour out My Spirit in those days; And they shall prophesy.

19 I will show wonders in heaven above and signs in the earth beneath: Blood and fire and vapor of smoke.

20 The sun shall be turned into darkness, And the moon into blood, Before the coming of the great and awesome day of the LORD.

21 And it shall come to pass That whoever calls on the name of the LORD Shall be saved.'

22 "Men of Israel, hear these words: Jesus of Nazareth, a Man attested by God to you by miracles, wonders, and signs which God

did through Him in your midst, as you yourselves also know--

God wants to restore to man all He gave to Adam in the beginning.

Get set for this is your moment of restoration and glory.

CHAPTER 5

HEALING ALL THE SICK VIA THE LIVING WORD

God wants all healed and delivered and restored.

In Psalms 107:20 it is written "He sent His word and healed them, and delivered them from their destructions." This Scripture makes healing compulsory for every preacher and everyone who teaches or preaches the Word of God.

Every Word from God must make man free from all sicknesses and diseases.

Please listen to me: Every Word from God's mouth is to make man and restore the image and likeness of God in man.

Proverbs 13:17 says "A faithful Ambassador is health!"

That makes Healing God's Greatest and Highest or Topmost priority.

And every faithful Ambassador made like God and sent as His Ambassador to shepherd His flock and sheep must partner with God our Father to make man in God's image and likeness. This makes healing our greatest, highest and topmost priority. And it takes being like God to Bring healing like God to the sick.

Proverbs 4:18- The path of the righteous is like a shinning light that shines brighter and brighter until the perfect day.

Proverbs 12:28- In the way of righteousness there is life; along that path is immortality.

Why is it so?

Psalms 97:3- Fire goes before him (The Lord) and consumes his foes on every side.

It is the Lord that goes before me. Fire goes before Him and consumes his foes on every side. Therefore, as I come behind him, following in His footsteps, all I see is a path that shines brighter and brighter with life and immortality on every side because all the evils have been consumed.

Isaiah 9:19 says the people [the wicked foes] will be fuel for the fire [as the fire goes before Him].

Daniel 7:10- A river of fire was flowing, coming out from before him.

Zechariah 1:19 –The fire devours the pastures and burn up the trees.

Joel 2:3- Before them [Ambassadors or God's army] fire devours, behind them a flame blazes.

Habakkuk 3:5-Plagues went before Him, pestilence followed His steps.

Notice according to Revelation 19:12-16 that the Word of God produces FIRE. Speaking about Jesus the Living Word made flesh, it is written, "His eyes were like a flame of fire, and on His head were many crowns. He had a name written that no one knew except Himself. He was clothed with a robe dipped in blood, and His name is called The Word of God. And the armies in heaven, clothed in fine linen, white and clean, followed Him on white horses. Now out of His mouth goes a sharp sword, that with it He should strike the nations. And He Himself will rule them with a rod of iron. He Himself treads the winepress of the fierceness and wrath of Almighty God. And He has on His robe and on His thigh a name written: KING OF KINGS AND LORD OF LORDS."

Sources of this fire!

2Samuel 22:9- Smoke rose from his nostrils; <u>consuming fire</u> came from his mouth.

That is through The Living Word burning coals blazed out of it.

Psalms 50:3- Our God comes and will not be silent (He'll Speak), a Fire devours before him.

Hebrews 12:29- Our God is a consuming fire. God and His Word IS one. So, The Living Word is Fire!

Revelation 11:5-6- If anyone lives to harm them, fire comes from the mouth of His witnesses and devours their enemies. This is how they must die.

These men have power to shut up the sky so that it will not rain during the time they are prophesying and speaking.

The effect of the fire is to consume whatever stands in the way of the chosen and sent Ambassadors to hinder them from exploits.

"Then one of the seraphim flew to me, having in his hand a live coal which he had taken with the tongs from the altar. And he touched my mouth with it, and said: "Behold, this has touched your lips; Your iniquity is taken away, And your sin purged. Also I heard the voice of the Lord, saying: "Whom shall I send, And who will go for Us?" Then I said, "Here am I! Send me." And He said, "Go, and tell this people: 'Keep on hearing, but do not understand; Keep on seeing, but do not perceive.' "Make the heart of this people dull, And their ears heavy, And shut their eyes; Lest they see with their eyes, And hear with their ears, And understand with their heart, And return and be healed." Then I said, "Lord, how long?" And He answered: "Until the cities are laid waste and without inhabitant, The houses are without a man, The land is utterly desolate, The LORD has removed men far away, And the forsaken places are many in the midst of the land. But yet a tenth will be in it, And will return and be for consuming, As a terebinth tree or as an oak, Whose stump remains when it is cut down. So the holy seed shall be its stump." Isaiah 6:6-13

The effect of the fire is for the purification of the chosen for a lifetime of impact and exploits

"Behold, I send My messenger, And he will prepare the way before Me. And the Lord, whom you seek, Will suddenly come to His temple, Even the Messenger of the covenant, In whom you delight. Behold, He is coming," Says the LORD of hosts. But who can endure the day of His coming? And who can stand when He appears? For He is like a refiner's fire And like launderer's soap. He will sit as a refiner and a purifier of silver; He will purify the sons of Levi, And purge them as gold and silver, That they may offer to the LORD An offering in righteousness." Malachi 3:1-3

The effect of the fire destroys our enemies and foes.

"Therefore, thus says the LORD God of hosts: "Because you speak this word, Behold, I will make My words in your mouth fire, And this people wood, And it shall devour them." Jeremiah 5:14

"And you shall know that I am the LORD; for you have not walked in My statutes nor executed My judgments, but have done according to the customs of the Gentiles which are all around you.'" Now it happened, while I was prophesying, that Pelatiah the son of Benaiah died. Then I fell on my face and cried with a loud voice, and said, "Ah, Lord GOD! Will You make a complete end of the remnant of Israel?" Ezekiel 1:12-13

The Living Word produces His fire that consumes sicknesses and diseases and All evils within the Temple of The Most High God – whose Temple you are.

"Then He spoke to the man clothed with linen, and said, "Go in among the wheels, under the cherub, fill your hands with coals of fire from among the cherubim, and scatter them over the city." And he went in as I watched. Now the cherubim were standing on the south side of the temple when the man went in, and the cloud filled the inner court. Then the glory of the LORD went up from the cherub, and paused over the threshold of the temple; and the house was filled with the cloud, and the court was full of the brightness of the LORD'S glory.

The Word of God is a fire – fire that never says it is enough until all the evil sicknesses and diseases and plantings of the devil are completely wiped off and away.

Every God sent Messenger and Ambassador of Christ is to be a flame of fire to serve this purpose.

Hebrews 1:7 says "And of the angels He says: "Who makes His angels spirits And His ministers a flame of fire."

Every true shepherd is to be a flame of fire!

CHAPTER 6

HEALING: DESTROY THE CAUSE AND THE EFFECT

To every effect, there is a cause.

To stop the effect, stop the cause.

Sickness has a cause. Therefore, to stop sickness, stop the cause.

Isaiah 53:4-5

4 "Surely he hath borne our griefs, and carried our sorrows: yet we did esteem him stricken, smitten of God, and afflicted.

5 But he was wounded for our transgressions, he was bruised for our iniquities: the chastisement of our peace was upon him; and with his stripes we are healed."

Matthew 8:17

"That it might be fulfilled which was spoken by Esaias the prophet, saying, Himself took our infirmities, and bare our sicknesses."

Isaiah is fulfilled.

1 Peter 2:24

"Who his own self bare our sins in his own body on the tree, that we, being dead to sins, should live unto righteousness: by whose stripes ye were healed."

1 Peter 2:24 shows how Jesus fulfilled the prophecy of Isaiah in Matthew 8:17.

He destroyed and removed the cause of sickness which is sin. And when Jesus carried away our sin in His own body on the tree. He took away all our sicknesses and diseases. Therefore, whatsoever He redeems also must be free-

"Christ has redeemed us from the curse of the law, having become a curse for us (for it is written, "Cursed is everyone who hangs on a tree"), that the blessing of Abraham might come upon the Gentiles in Christ Jesus, that we might receive the promise of the Spirit through faith." Galatians 3:13-14

According to Deuteronomy 28:58-61, every sickness and every disease known and unknown are all part of the curse.

"If you do not carefully observe all the words of this law that are written in this book, that you may fear this glorious and awesome name, THE LORD YOUR GOD, then the LORD will bring upon you and your descendants extraordinary plagues-great and prolonged plagues-and serious and prolonged sicknesses. Moreover, He will bring back on you all the diseases of Egypt, of which you were afraid, and they shall cling to you. Also, every sickness and every plague, which is not written in this Book of the Law, will the LORD bring upon you until you are destroyed."

Jesus came as The Living Word made flesh (John 1:14) to heal and deliver mankind from every sickness and every disease meant as Satan's weapon to destroy man (Psalms 107:20). And He accomplished His mission before He went back to heaven.

The Lord is Still our Healer today (Exodus 15:26) and He will heal forever (see Hebrews 13:8).

He has dealt with the cause. We are no longer supposed to experience the effect. To be free and live free, we must take our prescribed MEDICINE ALWAYS as directed (Galatians 3:13; Romans 10:8-10; Proverbs 4:20-23).

Some Medical students I know in Enugu State University of Science and Technology College of Medicine have spent 7 to 9 years studying medicine. They were yet to graduate as at the time of writing. If you sit down at The Master's feet and settle down to study and learn from God's medicine Book for 7 to 9 years, I don't think there is any sickness or disease that will be brought to you that will not be healed.

Proverbs 4:22 says His word is MEDICINE to All their flesh.

That simply means, there is nothing in any part of man's life The Living Word cannot heal.

The Living Word Heals all sicknesses and diseases no matter which part of a man's life the evil sickness or disease may be hiding.

"For the word of God is living and powerful, and sharper than any two-edged sword, piercing even to the division of soul and spirit, and of joints and marrow, and is a discerner of the thoughts and intents of the heart. And there is no creature hidden from His sight, but all things are naked and open to the eyes of Him to whom we must give account." Hebrews 4:12-13

The cause has been taken away. Therefore, the effect can no longer be in place.

This is why every trace of sickness and disease among the people is illegal and must not be seen around us.

Every true and relevant shepherd understands this truth or learns it and goes forth to set free all the diseased, sick, weak, driven away, lost sheep that have become cheap prey and spoils to the evil one.

CHAPTER 7

VISION AND HEALING

Healing and Health Centre
Proverbs 29:18
"Where there is no vision, the people perish: but he that keepeth the law, happy is he."

Without Vision people perish.

Sickness and disease cause and make people to perish.

Therefore, when a man is sick and diseased, a new vision of healing and health perfectly restored to him is to be shown to him. And that may be all he needs to be healed and live in health. If they can be helped and made to see a clear picture of who they can be and are meant to be in Christ, nothing will stop their healing and restoration to health.

Vision can facilitate and guarantee a man to be healed and restored to health and live. With a vision or the right picture painted, the sick can and will be made to live. Give them a new vision. Refocus and redirect them to see a brighter tomorrow and a glorious healthy body free from sickness and disease and they will have it.

Dr Bernie Siegel, a Medical Doctor told the story of John Flord in his new book, "Peace, Love and Healing."

John, a landscape gardener was diagnosed with cancer of the stomach and was advised to go for a surgery immediately. John told his doctor, "You forget surgery. It's springtime. I'm a landscape gardener, and I want to make the world beautiful that way if I survive, it's a gift. If I don't, I will have left a beautiful world." He had a vision and was willing to live for it or die fulfilling it.

Four weeks later he had surgery. Reports revealed that he still had a lot of cancer left in his body after the surgery.

Seven of his lymph nodes were positive for cancer- His doctor advised chemotherapy and X-ray therapy. But the doctors had forgotten his vision. It was bigger than his cancer. He told them, "It's still spring. I don't have time for all that treatment." He was at peace and he healed rapidly.

Four years later he returned for a check-up. He needed a hernia repaired. His cancer was completely gone.

John recently celebrated his 83rd birthday. As Dr. Siegel puts it, "You have to wonder-what happened to his cancer?"

Without a vision people perish. And with a vision people can and will live.

With a new vision of healing and health YOU can live!

Now is the time to cast down all those images of sickness and gloom.

What do you see?

"Then the LORD put forth His hand and touched my mouth, and the LORD said to me: "Behold, I have put My words in your mouth. See, I have this day set you over the nations and over the kingdoms, to root out and to pull down, to destroy and to throw down, to build and to plant." Moreover, the word of the LORD came to me, saying, "Jeremiah, **what do you see?"** And I said, "I see a branch of an almond tree." **Then the LORD said to me, "You have seen well**, for I am ready to perform My word." Jeremiah 1:9-12

The truth is that the Lord says, WHATEVER you have seen, YO HAVE SEEN WELL!

And based on what you have seen, The LORD will HASTEN His Word to perform it.

True and relevant shepherds may be one (1) in a thousand but they paint pictures and show the diseased flock the new vision of the Lord who TOOK and CARRIED away all their sins and sicknesses. And by so doing, free them from every sickness and disease.

"Man is also chastened with pain on his bed, and with strong pain in many of his bones, so that his life abhors bread, And his soul succulent food. His flesh wastes away from sight, and his bones stick out which once were not seen. Yes, his soul draws near the Pit, and his life to the executioners. "If there is a messenger for him, A mediator, one among a thousand, To show man His uprightness, Then He is gracious to him, and says, 'Deliver him from going down to the Pit; I have found a ransom'; His flesh shall be young like a child's, He shall return to the days of his youth." Job 33:19-25

Vision is a powerful force. You need it to safeguard your life against sickness and disease.

CHAPTER 8

3-IN-1 KILLER DIS-EASE IN THE
'CHURCH' AND WHAT YOU
MUST DO ABOUT THEM

It is written "Then the scribes and Pharisees who were from Jerusalem came to Jesus, saying, "Why do Your disciples transgress the tradition of the elders? For they do not wash their hands when they eat bread." He answered and said to them, "Why do you also transgress the commandment of God because of your tradition? "For God commanded, saying, 'Honor your father and your mother'; and, 'He who curses father or mother, let him be put to death.' "But you say, 'Whoever says to his father or mother, "Whatever profit you might have received from me is a gift to God" --'then he need not honor his father or mother.' Thus, you have made the commandment of God of no effect by your tradition." Matthew 15:1-6

The people of Israel said 'Whoever says to his father or mother, "Whatever profit you might have received from me is a gift to God, and honour not his father or his mother, he shall be free.' And the Lord said "Thus have you made the commandment of God of none effect by your tradition."

Mark 7:12-13

12 "And ye suffer him no more to do ought for his father or his mother;

13 Making the word of God of none effect through your tradition, which ye have delivered: and many such like things do ye."

There is a 3 in 1 killer disease in the church and among Christians that have clamed more lives than any terminal disease in the history of mankind.

It is called TRADITION, and it has 3 branches-

1. **It is not always God's will to heal.**

The first tradition-killer dis-ease says it is not always God's will to heal you.

It is a lie. Yet so many have believed it.

It is always God's will to heal you. Healing is the children's bread.

Notice Matthew 15:1-6 and compare it with Matthew 15:21-28.

Also notice Mark 7:12-13 and compare it with Mark 7:24-30.

Matthew 15:21-28

21 ¶ Then Jesus went out from there and departed to the region of Tyre and Sidon.

22 And behold, a woman of Canaan came from that region and cried out to Him, saying, "Have mercy on me, O Lord, Son of David! My daughter is severely demon-possessed."

23 But He answered her not a word. And His disciples came and urged Him, saying, "Send her away, for she cries out after us."

24 But He answered and said, "I was not sent except to the lost sheep of the house of Israel."

25 Then she came and worshiped Him, saying, "Lord, help me!"

26 But He answered and said, "It is not good to take the children's bread and throw it to the little dogs."

27 And she said, "Yes, Lord, yet even the little dogs eat the crumbs which fall from their masters' table."

28 Then Jesus answered and said to her, "O woman, great is your faith! Let it be to you as you desire." And her daughter was healed from that very hour.

Mark 7:24-30

24 ¶ From there He arose and went to the region of Tyre and Sidon. And He entered a house and wanted no one to know it, but

He could not be hidden.

25 For a woman whose young daughter had an unclean spirit heard about Him, and she came and fell at His feet.

26 The woman was a Greek, a Syro-Phoenician by birth, and she kept asking Him to cast the demon out of her daughter.

27 But Jesus said to her, "Let the children be filled first, for it is not good to take the children's bread and throw it to the little dogs."

28 And she answered and said to Him, "Yes, Lord, yet even the little dogs under the table eat from the children's crumbs."

29 Then He said to her, "For this saying go your way; the demon has gone out of your daughter."

30 And when she had come to her house, she found the demon gone out, and her daughter lying on the bed.

2. <u>Healing has passed away.</u>

The second is also a cruel tradition that has caged even most "believing" pastors. They now have their doctors, their family doctors; children's doctors; consultants' doctors etc. When church members are sick, Pastors refer them to doctors or name drugs they must get to be free. It is evil. So many Christians have died because of this wicked killer disease in the body of Christ.

Until heaven ends and earth passes away, healing cannot end nor pass away.

Heaven and earth will pass away, but not a title of the word will pass away.

The Living Word He sent cannot pass away.

Psalms 107:20 says He sent His and Healed and delivered the sick from their sicknesses and diseases and evil destructions.

For as long as we have the God's Word, healing cannot pass away.

The Lord's Covenant Name is "The Lord That Heals You!

It is written in Exodus 15:26 "And said, If thou wilt diligently hearken to the voice of the LORD thy God, and wilt do that which is right in his sight, and wilt give ear to his commandments, and keep all his statutes, I will put none of these diseases upon thee, which I have brought upon the Egyptians: for I am the LORD that healeth thee."

"For I am the LORD, I change not; therefore, ye sons of Jacob are not consumed." Malachi 3:6

Exodus 3:14 "And God said unto Moses, I AM THAT I AM: and he said, thus shalt thou say unto the children of Israel, I AM hath sent me unto you."

Hebrews 13:8 "Jesus Christ the same yesterday, and to day, and for ever."

3. <u>God gets glory when Christians are sick</u>

This is the most dangerous tradition - that God gets glory when Christians are sick or are being attacked by Satan with sickness and disease. It is a lie.

Your healing gets God glory.

The multitude glorified God when the daughter of Abraham Satan bound for 18 years got healed.

"Now He was teaching in one of the synagogues on the Sabbath. And behold, there was a woman who had a spirit of infirmity eighteen years, and was bent over and could in no way raise herself up. But when Jesus saw her, He called her to Him and said to her, "Woman, you are loosed from your infirmity." And He laid His hands on her, and immediately she was made straight, and glorified God. But the ruler of the synagogue answered with indignation, because Jesus had healed on the Sabbath; and he said to the crowd, "There are six days on which men ought to work; therefore, come and be healed on them, and not on the Sabbath day." The Lord then answered him and said, "Hypocrite! Does not each one of you on the Sabbath lose his ox or donkey from the stall, and lead it away to water it? "So, ought not this woman, being a daughter of Abraham, whom Satan has bound--think of it--for eighteen years, be loosed from this bond on the Sabbath?" And when He said these things, all His adversaries were put to shame; and all the multitude rejoiced for all the glorious things that were done by Him." Luke 13:10-17

The people praised and glorified God when the lame man got healed.

Now Peter and John went up together to the temple at the

hour of prayer, the ninth hour. And a certain man lame from his mother's womb was carried, whom they laid daily at the gate of the temple which is called Beautiful, to ask alms from those who entered the temple; who, seeing Peter and John about to go into the temple, asked for alms. And fixing his eyes on him, with John, Peter said, "Look at us." So, he gave them his attention, expecting to receive something from them. Then Peter said, "Silver and gold I do not have, but what I do have I give you: In the name of Jesus Christ of Nazareth, rise up and walk. And he took him by the right hand and lifted him up, and immediately his feet and ankle bones received strength. So, he, leaping up, stood and walked and entered the temple with them--walking, leaping, and praising God. And all the people saw him walking and praising God." Acts 3:1-9

The people glorified God when the paralytic got healed.

"However, the report went around concerning Him all the more; and great multitudes came together to hear, and to be healed by Him of their infirmities. So, He Himself often withdrew into the wilderness and prayed. Now it happened on a certain day, as He was teaching, that there were Pharisees and teachers of the law sitting by, who had come out of every town of Galilee, Judea, and Jerusalem. And the power of the Lord was present to heal them. Then behold, men brought on a bed a man who was paralyzed, whom they sought to bring in and lay before Him. And when they could not find how they might bring him in, because of the crowd, they went up on the housetop and let him down with his bed through the tiling into the midst before Jesus. When He saw their faith, He said to him, "Man, your sins are forgiven you." And the scribes and the Pharisees began to reason, saying, "Who is this who speaks blasphemies? Who can forgive sins but God alone?" But when Jesus perceived their thoughts, He answered and said to them, "Why are you reasoning in your hearts? "Which is easier, to say, 'Your sins are forgiven you,' or to say, 'Rise up and walk'? "But that you may know that the Son of Man has power on earth to forgive sins" --He said to the man who was paralyzed, "I say to you, arise, take up your bed, and go to your house." Immediately he rose up before them, took up what he had been lying on, and departed to his own house, glorifying God. And they were all amazed, and they glorified God and were filled with fear, saying, "We have seen strange things today!". Luke 5:15-26

The world is looking for a way out of sickness and disease, not a way into it.

Let's break down those traditions and deliver a hurting world from the most dangerous killer of all-Traditions - RELIGIOUS TRADITION. (Matthew 15:6; Mark 7:12-13).

HOW DO WE DO IT?

1.Teach and uphold Faith and not tradition.

Matthew 15:21-28

21 ¶ Then Jesus went out from there and departed to the region of Tyre and Sidon.

22 And behold, a woman of Canaan came from that region and cried out to Him, saying, "Have mercy on me, O Lord, Son of David! My daughter is severely demon-possessed."

23 But He answered her not a word. And His disciples came and urged Him, saying, "Send her away, for she cries out after us."

24 But He answered and said, **"I was not sent except to the lost sheep of the house of Israel."**

25 Then she came and worshiped Him, saying, "Lord, help me!"

26 But He answered and said, "It is not good to take the children's bread and throw it to the little dogs."

27 And she said, "Yes, Lord, yet even the little dogs eat the crumbs which fall from their masters' table."

28 **Then Jesus answered and said to her, "O woman, great is your faith! Let it be to you as you desire." And her daughter was healed from that very hour.**

Jesus was sent to the lost sheep of the house of Israel (Matthew 15:24)

Yet He broke it because of faith and healed the stranger to the covenant.

2. Teach and Honour the Faith Confession of those who Understand God's Word and Believes it will work for them.

Mark 7:24-30

24 ¶ From there He arose and went to the region of Tyre and

Sidon. And He entered a house and wanted no one to know it, but He could not be hidden.

25 For a woman whose young daughter had an unclean spirit heard about Him, and she came and fell at His feet.

26 The woman was a Greek, a Syro-Phoenician by birth, and she kept asking Him to cast the demon out of her daughter.

27 But Jesus said to her, "Let the children be filled first, for it is not good to take the children's bread and throw it to the little dogs."

28 And she answered and said to Him, "Yes, Lord, yet even the little dogs under the table eat from the children's crumbs."

29 Then He said to her, **"For this saying go your way; the demon has gone out of your daughter**."

30 And when she had come to her house, she found the demon gone out, and her daughter lying on the bed.

Jesus was sent to care for God's children first and He said to her, **"Let the children be filled first, for it is not good to take the children's bread and throw it to the little dogs."**

Yet when the woman confessed her faith in the crumbs KNOWING that the bread from the master's table and the crumbs were made up of the same nutrients and that **size was not the issue but the content**.

And Jesus had no choice than to break the tradition of feeding the children first and met that woman's need first.

The mysteries of the Kingdom are here for all of mankind. All who understand them are qualified for healing and every other blessing

"And the disciples came and said to Him, "Why do You speak to them in parables?" He answered and said to them, "Because it has been given to you to know the mysteries of the kingdom of heaven, but to them it has not been given. "For whoever has, to him more will be given, and he will have abundance; but whoever does not have, even what he has will be taken away from him. "Therefore, I speak to them in parables, because seeing they do not see, and hearing they do not hear, nor do they understand. "And in them the prophecy of Isaiah is fulfilled, which says: 'Hearing you will hear and shall not understand, and seeing you will see and not perceive; For the hearts of this people have grown dull. Their ears are hard of hearing, and their eyes they have closed, lest they should see with their eyes and hear with their ears, lest they should understand with their hearts and turn, so that I should heal them." Matthew 13:10-15

Good and relevant shepherds open the understanding of the people as Jesus did to His disciples. And feed them with knowledge and understanding until there is no lack among them.

It is written "And I will give you shepherds according to My heart, who will feed you with knowledge and understanding. Then it shall come to pass, when you are multiplied and increased in the land in those days," says the LORD, "that they will say no more, 'The ark of the covenant of the LORD.' It shall not come to mind, nor shall they remember it, nor shall they visit it, nor shall it be made anymore." Jeremiah 3:15-16

Luke 24:45 says "And He [Jesus] opened their understanding, that they might comprehend the Scriptures."

Feed them with knowledge and understanding until there is no lack among them.

CHAPTER 9

HEAL AND LIBERATE ALL EVERYDAY, EVERYWHERE!

Jesus was consistent in His Message and Ministry to those The Father sent Him!

The summary of the ministry of Jesus Christ is written in Acts 10:36-38 "The word which God sent to the children of Israel, preaching peace through Jesus Christ--He is Lord of all--"that word you know, which was proclaimed throughout all Judea, and began from Galilee after the baptism which John preached: "how God anointed Jesus of Nazareth with the Holy Spirit and with power, who went about doing good and healing all who were oppressed by the devil, for God was with Him."

Scripture records in Matthew 9:35 and 4:23-25 what Jesus did every day, everywhere He went!

"Then Jesus went about all the cities and villages, teaching in their synagogues, preaching the gospel of the kingdom, and healing every sickness and every disease among the people."

"And Jesus went about all Galilee, teaching in their synagogues, preaching the gospel of the kingdom, and healing all kinds of sickness and all kinds of disease among the people. Then His fame went throughout all Syria; and they brought to Him all sick people who were afflicted with various diseases and torments, and those who were demon-possessed, epileptics, and paralytics;

and He healed them. Great multitudes followed Him--from Galilee, and from Decapolis, Jerusalem, Judea, and beyond the Jordan."

Notice in Luke 4:16-27, we see Jesus announce His mandate and mission and declared it was to happen everyday of This Jubilee Year – that is, Till He Returns!

16 "And he came to Nazareth, where he had been brought up: and, as his custom was, he went into the synagogue on the sabbath day, and stood up for to read.

17 And there was delivered unto him the book of the prophet Esaias. And when he had opened the book, he found the place where it was written,

18 The Spirit of the Lord is upon me, because he hath anointed me to preach the gospel to the poor; he hath sent me to heal the brokenhearted, to preach deliverance to the captives, and recovering of sight to the blind, to set at liberty them that are bruised,

19 To preach the acceptable year of the Lord.

20 And he closed the book, and he gave it again to the minister, and sat down. And the eyes of all them that were in the synagogue were fastened on him.

21 And he began to say unto them, this day is this scripture fulfilled in your ears.

22 And all bare him witness, and wondered at the gracious words which proceeded out of his mouth. And they said, Is not this Joseph's son?"

23 He said to them, "You will surely say this proverb to Me, 'Physician, heal yourself! Whatever we have heard done in Capernaum, do also here in Your country.'"

24 Then He said, "Assuredly, I say to you, no prophet is accepted in his own country.

25 "But I tell you truly, many widows were in Israel in the days of Elijah, when the heaven was shut up three years and six months, and there was a great famine throughout all the land;

26 "but to none of them was Elijah sent except to Zarephath, in the region of Sidon, to a woman who was a widow.

27 "And many lepers were in Israel in the time of Elisha the

prophet, and none of them was cleansed except Naaman the Syrian."

Jesus announced His Purpose to them and to all: He had come to liberate ALL of mankind from all evil holds. Men and women are to be free from all captivity and restored to their possession and to their father's family as stated by God through the mouth of His prophet Moses in Leviticus 25:10. And He began it from that day in Nazareth.

And every day, wherever Jesus went He did the same. Acts 10:38 says Jesus went everywhere doing good and Healing all that were oppressed by the devil until the end of his time on earth. And after His resurrection from death, He spent 40 days speaking to His disciples of things pertaining to the Kingdom. That means, He taught them on all He did and How to continue doing the same works He did.

Jesus taught on the same kingdom matters that God gave nan in Genesis 1:26-28!

Notice Acts 1:1-2: After His resurrection, Jesus continued from where He had stopped until He was taken to Heaven after instructing His disciples to continue from where He stopped. Notice also that Jesus went everywhere Healing and liberating men and women (Acts 10:38; Matthew 9:35; 4:23-25; etc).

The apostles also did same. Luke 9:6; Mark 16:20.

Paul also did-Romans 15:18-20; Acts 19:11-12; 2Corinthians 12:12.

The Church was commissioned to do likewise (Mathew 28:18-20; Acts 1:8; Mark 16:15-18).

That shows very clearly that Healing and Liberating mankind is to be done today, and every day everywhere man is found. If nothing could stop them wherever they went as apostles from doing Healing and Liberating all, then there is nothing that is to stop me and everyone else that will believe and step out by faith today. Healing and Liberating men and women is to be done daily, everywhere.

Jesus began it, the apostles continued it. We are to bring it to the end of the world. We are to it until Jesus Christ returns.

Jesus told the apostles to begin Healing and Liberating men and women from Jerusalem, then continue same in Judea, continue it in Samaria (the Isolated ones) and then continue same to the ends of the earth.

He was aware of medical science yet He told us to heal and liberate all from all Satanic oppressions.

That is why I am here and that is what I am going to do. And there is nothing that will stop us.

A sister in Institute of Management Technology just died. Her life was cut short by the devil. Had I started my work; she might not have died but could have lived. That is why we must take-off to bring healing to the sick. We must start to organize meetings and teach Healing ∞ as He commanded me.

<u>IT IS GOD'S WILL TO HEAL TODAY BECAUSE HE IS THE I AM THAT HEALED IN THE PAST.</u>

How can The Lord Jesus Christ Heal All who are oppressed by the same devil today?

Philippians 2:13

"For it is God which worketh in you both to will and to do of his good pleasure."

It is God that works in me BOTH TO WILL and to do (work) His works.

Therefore, since it is His will to HEAL TODAY, it is His will TO DO (HEALING) THROUGH ME TODAY.

Therefore, He will Do/Work Healing through me.

Daniel 11:38

"But in his estate shall he honour **the God of forces**:" (KJV)

God is called "the God of forces". He is the head and controller of all forces. That is why I cannot be stopped.

The Lord wants all Healed. It is His will to Heal All. So, all will be Healed.

If All are not healed, it is never His fault. The fault is <u>OURS</u> and ours alone. God is never to be blamed for anyone's inability to receive his/her healing. The problem(s) is man's and he is to be blamed.

2/3 of the worlds are not privileged to have medical science and treatment made available to them.

80% of people in Africa do not have access to even elementary medical care.

Even in the advanced countries, medical science is failing so many and also is not within the reach of everyone.

Presently, about 95 percent of the world's population are sick.

This is why I must Dive into this ministry the Lord personally handed over to me with All in me.

Healing is not a secondary issue. Healing is primary. Healing is fundamental. Healing is Heaven's topmost priority.

On 7-1-2012, the Lord said to me "Heals Zillion!" He wrote it also and gave it to me.

Two days later, on the 9-1-2012, The Lord appeared to me again and said "Your Job description is Acts 10:38: Do good to all and heal all that are oppressed of the devil!"

I have been given ministry in a wholesale land scale (earth) proportion. Even the most advanced nations need the Healing power of Christ in me. I must not delay anymore.

WHY I MUST HEAL ALL

1.Jesus healed as Christ the Messiah (or Anointed and Sent one).

And I have His Spirit and Anointing in and on Me! Romans 8:9,11

John 17:18,20-21

18 "As thou hast sent me into the world, even so have I also sent them into the world.

20 Neither pray I for these alone, but for them also which shall believe on me through their word;

21 That they all may be one; as thou, Father, art in me, and I in thee, that they also may be one in us: that the world may believe that thou hast sent me."

2Corinthians 1:20-21 "For all the promises of God in him are yea, and in him Amen, unto the glory of God by us. Now he which stablisheth us with you in Christ, and hath anointed us, is God."

2. Jesus healed as the Prophet (Speaker of The Living Word).

Matthew 8:16

"When the even was come, they brought unto him many that were possessed with devils: and he cast out the spirits with his word, and healed all that were sick:"

John 17:18

"As thou hast sent me into the world, even so have I also sent them into the world."

John 20:21

"Then said Jesus to them again, Peace be unto you: as my Father hath sent me, even so send I you."

Psalms 107:20

"He sent his word, and healed them, and delivered them from their destructions."

Via the Living Word, I am to do as He did. The Living Word was the channel of His healings.

3. Jesus healed because he had compassion on them (Love). Drawn by love, I'm to do as He did.

1John 3:23

"And this is his commandment, that we should believe on the name of his Son Jesus Christ, and love one another, as he gave us commandment."

4. Jesus healed because he is the Son of God.

John 10:34-36

34 "Jesus answered them, is it not written in your law, I said, Ye are gods?

35 If he called them gods, unto whom the word of God came, and the scripture cannot be broken;

36 Say ye of him, whom the Father hath sanctified, and sent into the world, thou blasphemest; because I said, I am the Son of God?"

I am God's son as Jesus is.

Romans 8:29

"For whom he did foreknow, he also did predestinate to be conformed to the image of his Son, that he might be the firstborn among many brethren."

Galatians 4:6-7

6 "And because ye are sons, God hath sent forth the Spirit of his

Son into your hearts, crying, Abba, Father.

7 Wherefore thou art no more a servant, but a son; and if a son, then an heir of God through Christ."

I am to heal also as the son of God.

The Messiah (sent one) is to heal the sick ones.

The Preacher, Teacher, Speaker, Minister of the Lord is to speak The Living Word which is to be confirmed by His living healing action-Psalms 107:20; Mark 16:20. heal the sick.

Love will never pass by human need and ignore/do nothing about it. Love will never fail to meet human needs.

5. Jesus Healed by the Anointing. Isaiah 10:27; Acts 10:38

The Son of God carries an anointing to heal all the sick. 1John 2:20,27

"And it shall come to pass in that day, that his burden shall be taken away from off thy shoulder, and his yoke from off thy neck, and the yoke shall be destroyed because of the anointing."

Luke 4:18-19

18 "The Spirit of the Lord is upon me, because he hath anointed me to preach the gospel to the poor; he hath sent me to heal the brokenhearted, to preach deliverance to the captives, and re-covering of sight to the blind, to set at liberty them that are bruised,

19 To preach the acceptable year of the Lord."

Acts 10:38

"How God anointed Jesus of Nazareth with the Holy Ghost and with power: who went about doing good, and healing all that were oppressed of the devil; for God was with him."

John 17:18

"As thou hast sent me into the world, even so have I also sent them into the world."

John 20:21

"Then said Jesus to them again, Peace be unto you: as my Father hath sent me, even so send I you."

John 14:12

"Verily, verily, I say unto you, He that believeth on me, the works that I do shall he do also; and greater works than these shall he do; because I go unto my Father."

I will set them free in Jesus Name.

-Jesus is conqueror.

Proclaim liberty and restoration to the captives throughout all the land to all the inhabitants thereof. Go into all the world and tell men that are bound mentally, spiritually, physically, emotionally, the liberator has come (in my person-Philippians 2:13).

- Leviticus 25:10

"And ye shall hallow the fiftieth year, and proclaim liberty throughout all the land unto all the inhabitants thereof: it shall be a jubilee unto you; and ye shall return every man unto his possession, and ye shall return every man unto his family." Proclaim liberty throughout the land (Earth)

- Jesus liberated men and women from All that oppressed them and from sicknesses and diseases, satanic powers, death, bad economy etc.

Men and women are in bondage to fear, the future, poverty, sickness etc and so need freedom and liberty.

Many are suffering today under economic oppressions. They are "Economically oppressed" I must also liberate them in the Name of Jesus.

People are mentally oppressed, spiritually oppressed, physically oppressed, economically oppressed, educationally and academically oppressed, socially oppressed, and financially oppressed. Go and liberate them. Jesus cane as the liberator (Luke 4:16-27; Isaiah 61:1-2; Acts 10:38).

He sent me in His stead now. He has anointed me as He was and sent me as the liberator now. Henceforth, captives were going to be released and the oppressed set and go free. An end has come to every sickness and disease, Satan and sin, death and the destroyer, and to the grave and the law (the tyrant).

Conquer the strong man and then release his prisoners.

Colossians 2:15- Jesus the liberator came and conquered. He has sent me to proclaim this message throughout the earth.

I must stop all the Economic oppressors, mental oppressors,

spiritual or religious oppressors, physical oppressors, financial oppressors and release their captives and set free their oppressed ones. Heal and deliver all. Restore all.

This is the duty of His relevant shepherds!

CHAPTER 10

The Everlasting Gospel is the Power of God unto salvation - from sin, from sickness, from slavery (bondage), from suffering in poverty, from starvation, from selfishness, from Satan and from all evils to everyone that believes.

Plant the Seed and The Harvest Will Be Inevitable.

Until the seed of the gospel is sown, the harvest of salvation from the above is impossible, no matter the effort man puts in.

Psalms 103:2-7

2 "Bless the LORD, O my soul, and forget not all his benefits:

3 Who forgives all thine iniquities; who healeth all thy diseases;

4 Who redeems thy life from destruction; who crowneth thee with lovingkindness and tender mercies;

5 Who satisfies thy mouth with good things; so that thy youth is renewed like the eagle's.

6 ¶ The LORD executes righteousness and judgment for all that are oppressed.

7 He made known his ways unto Moses, his acts unto the children of Israel."

Remember all His benefits.

He forgives all your sins; He heals all your sicknesses. Before forgiveness of your sins (harvest), there is (the sowing of the seed) the message of salvation. It is important to always remember that until the message of salvation or gospel (seed) is planted, forgiveness of sins (harvest) is unattainable.

The same goes for healing of all your diseases. So many want to be healed by the Lord. They all must be ready and willing to hear the message of healing (seed sowing which brings the harvest they so much desire).

Mark 16:15-20

15 "And he said unto them, go ye into all the world, and preach the gospel to every creature.

16 He that believeth and is baptized shall be saved; but he that believeth not shall be damned.

17 And these signs shall follow them that believe; In my name shall they cast out devils; they shall speak with new tongues;

18 They shall take up serpents; and if they drink any deadly thing, it shall not hurt them; they shall lay hands on the sick, and they shall recover.

19 So then after the Lord had spoken unto them, he was received up into heaven, and sat on the right hand of God.

20 And they went forth, and preached every where, the Lord working with them, and confirming the word with signs following. Amen."

The message (seed) precedes the harvest outlined in the text.

James 5:14-16

14 "Is any sick among you? let him call for the elders of the church; and let them pray over him, anointing him with oil in the name of the Lord:

15 And the prayer of faith shall save the sick, and the Lord shall raise him up; and if he have committed sins, they shall be forgiven him.

16 Confess your faults one to another, and pray one for another, that ye may be healed. The effectual fervent prayer of a righteous man availeth much."

Being a member of the church, which shows that the sick has heard the message (have the seed in them) precedes anointing with oil and laying on of hands/praying the prayer of faith.

Mark 6:7-13

7 "And he called unto him the twelve, and began to send them forth by two and two; and gave them power over unclean spirits;

8 And commanded them that they should take nothing for their journey, save a staff only; no scrip, no bread, no money in their purse: {money: the word signifieth a piece of brass money, in value somewhat less than a farthing, but here it is taken in general for money}

9 But be shod with sandals; and not put on two coats.

10 And he said unto them, in what place soever ye enter into a house, there abide till ye depart from that place.

11 And whosoever shall not receive you, nor hear you, when ye depart thence, shake off the dust under your feet for a testimony against them. Verily I say unto you, it shall be more tolerable for Sodom and Gomorrah in the day of judgment, than for that city.

12 And they went out, and preached that men should repent.

13 And they cast out many devils, and anointed with oil many that were sick, and healed them."

Preaching (seed sowing) precedes healing the sick and casting out devils.

Luke 9:1-6

1 "Then he called his twelve disciples together, and gave them power and authority over all devils, and to cure diseases.

2 And he sent them to preach the kingdom of God, and to heal the sick.

3 And he said unto them, take nothing for your journey, neither staves, nor scrip, neither bread, neither money; neither have two coats apiece.

4 And whatsoever house ye enter into, there abide, and thence depart.

5 And whosoever will not receive you, when ye go out of that city, shake off the very dust from your feet for a testimony against them.

6 And they departed, and went through the towns, preaching the gospel, and healing every where."

Preaching (seed sowing) precedes healing.

Luke 10:1-9

1 "After these things the Lord appointed other seventy also, and sent them two and two before his face into every city and place, whither he himself would come.

2 Therefore said he unto them, the harvest truly is great, but the labourers are few: pray ye therefore the Lord of the harvest, that he would send forth labourers into his harvest.

3 Go your ways: behold, I send you forth as lambs among wolves.

4 Carry neither purse, nor scrip, nor shoes: and salute no man by the way.

5 And into whatsoever house ye enter, first say, Peace be to this house.

6 And if the son of peace be there, your peace shall rest upon it: if not, it shall turn to you again.

7 And in the same house remain, eating and drinking such things as they give: for the labourer is worthy of his hire. Go not from house to house.

8 And into whatsoever city ye enter, and they receive you, eat such things as are set before you:

9 And heal the sick that are therein, and say unto them, the kingdom of God is come nigh unto you."

Preaching (seed-sowing) precedes healing.

Acts 19:1-12

1 "And it came to pass, that, while Apollos was at Corinth, Paul having passed through the upper coasts came to Ephesus: and finding certain disciples,

2 He said unto them, have ye received the Holy Ghost since ye believed? And they said unto him, we have not so much as heard whether there be any Holy Ghost.

3 And he said unto them, unto what then were ye baptized? And they said, Unto John's baptism.

4 Then said Paul, John verily baptized with the baptism of repentance, saying unto the people, that they should believe on him which should come after him, that is, on Christ Jesus.

5 When they heard this, they were baptized in the name of the Lord Jesus.

6 And when Paul had laid his hands upon them, the Holy Ghost came on them; and they spake with tongues, and prophesied.

7 And all the men were about twelve.

8 And he went into the synagogue, and spake boldly for the space of three months, disputing and persuading the things concerning the kingdom of God.

9 But when divers were hardened, and believed not, but spake evil of that way before the multitude, he departed from them, and separated the disciples, disputing daily in the school of one Tyrannus.

10 And this continued by the space of two years; so that all they which dwelt in Asia heard the word of the Lord Jesus, both Jews and Greeks.

11 And God wrought special miracles by the hands of Paul:

12 So that from his body were brought unto the sick handkerchiefs or aprons, and the diseases departed from them, and the evil spirits went out of them."

Preaching (seed-sowing) precedes healing

Acts 8:4-13

4 "Therefore they that were scattered abroad went every where preaching the word.

5 Then Philip went down to the city of Samaria, and preached Christ unto them.

6 And the people with one accord gave heed unto those things which Philip spake, hearing and seeing the miracles which he did.

7 For unclean spirits, crying with loud voice, came out of many that were possessed with them: and many taken with palsies, and that were lame, were healed.

8 And there was great joy in that city.

9 But there was a certain man, called Simon, which beforetime in the same city used sorcery, and bewitched the people of Samaria, giving out that himself was some great one:

10 To whom they all gave heed, from the least to the greatest, saying, this man is the great power of God.

11 And to him they had regard, because that of long time he had bewitched them with sorceries.

12 But when they believed Philip preaching the things concerning the kingdom of God, and the name of Jesus Christ, they were baptized, both men and women.

13 Then Simon himself believed also: and when he was baptized, he continued with Philip, and wondered, beholding the miracles and signs which were done."

Preaching (seed-sowing) precedes healing.

Proverbs 4:20-22

20 "My son, attend to my words; incline thine ear unto my sayings.

21 Let them not depart from thine eyes; keep them in the midst of thine heart.

22 For they are life unto those that find them, and health to all their flesh."

Sowing the seed precedes enjoying the life and health of the Lord.

Sow the seed and the harvest will be inevitable. Once you sow the seed, relax, nothing under heaven will stop the harvest of salvation from the 7 harvests above. The Lord cannot break His word (John 10:35; Genesis 8:22).

Luke 4:16-27

16 So He came to Nazareth, where He had been brought up. And as His custom was, He went into the synagogue on the Sabbath day, and stood up to read.

17 And He was handed the book of the prophet Isaiah. And when He had opened the book, He found the place where it was written:

18 "The Spirit of the LORD is upon Me, Because He has anointed Me To preach the gospel to the poor; He has sent Me to heal the brokenhearted, to proclaim liberty to the captives and recovery of sight to the blind, to set at liberty those who are oppressed;

19 To proclaim the acceptable year of the LORD."

20 Then He closed the book, and gave it back to the attendant and sat down. And the eyes of all who were in the synagogue were

fixed on Him.

21 And He began to say to them, "Today this Scripture is fulfilled in your hearing."

22 So all bore witness to Him, and marveled at the gracious words which proceeded out of His mouth. And they said, "Is this not Joseph's son?"

23 He said to them, "You will surely say this proverb to Me, 'Physician, heal yourself! Whatever we have heard done in Capernaum, do also here in Your country.'"

24 Then He said, "Assuredly, I say to you, no prophet is accepted in his own country.

25 "But I tell you truly, many widows were in Israel in the days of Elijah, when the heaven was shut up three years and six months, and there was a great famine throughout all the land;

26 "but to none of them was Elijah sent except to Zarephath, in the region of Sidon, to a woman who was a widow.

27 "And many lepers were in Israel in the time of Elisha the prophet, and none of them was cleansed except Naaman the Syrian."

Acts 10:36-38

36 The word which God sent unto the children of Israel, preaching peace by Jesus Christ: (he is Lord of all:)

37 That word, I say, ye know, which was published throughout all Judaea, and began from Galilee, after the baptism which John preached;

38 How God anointed Jesus of Nazareth with the Holy Ghost and with power: who went about doing good, and healing all that were oppressed of the devil; for God was with him.

Luke 5:15-26

15 However, the report went around concerning Him all the more; and great multitudes came together to hear, and to be healed by Him of their infirmities.

16 So He Himself often withdrew into the wilderness and prayed.

17 ¶ Now it happened on a certain day, as He was teaching, that there were Pharisees and teachers of the law sitting by, who had

come out of every town of Galilee, Judea, and Jerusalem. And the power of the Lord was present to heal them.

18 Then behold, men brought on a bed a man who was paralyzed, whom they sought to bring in and lay before Him.

19 And when they could not find how they might bring him in, because of the crowd, they went up on the housetop and let him down with his bed through the tiling into the midst before Jesus.

20 When He saw their faith, He said to him, "Man, your sins are forgiven you."

21 And the scribes and the Pharisees began to reason, saying, "Who is this who speaks blasphemies? Who can forgive sins but God alone?"

22 But when Jesus perceived their thoughts, He answered and said to them, "Why are you reasoning in your hearts?

23 "Which is easier, to say, 'Your sins are forgiven you,' or to say, 'Rise up and walk'?

24 "But that you may know that the Son of Man has power on earth to forgive sins" --He said to the man who was paralyzed, "I say to you, arise, take up your bed, and go to your house."

25 Immediately he rose up before them, took up what he had been lying on, and departed to his own house, glorifying God.

26 And they were all amazed, and they glorified God and were filled with fear, saying, "We have seen strange things today!"

Luke 6:17-19

17 And He came down with them and stood on a level place with a crowd of His disciples and a great multitude of people from all Judea and Jerusalem, and from the seacoast of Tyre and Sidon, who came to hear Him and be healed of their diseases,

18 as well as those who were tormented with unclean spirits. And they were healed.

19 And the whole multitude sought to touch Him, for power went out from Him and healed them all.

Matthew 9:35 And Jesus went about all the cities and villages, teaching in their synagogues, and preaching the gospel of the kingdom, and healing every sickness and every disease among the people.

Matthew 4:4:23-24

23 ¶ And Jesus went about all Galilee, teaching in their synagogues, and preaching the gospel of the kingdom, and healing all manner of sickness and all manner of disease among the people.

24 And his fame went throughout all Syria: and they brought unto him all sick people that were taken with divers' diseases and torments, and those which were possessed with devils, and those which were lunatick, and those that had the palsy; and he healed them.

Matthew 10:1-8

1 ¶ And when he had called unto him his twelve disciples, he gave them power against unclean spirits, to cast them out, and to heal all manner of sickness and all manner of disease.

2 Now the names of the twelve apostles are these; The first, Simon, who is called Peter, and Andrew his brother; James the son of Zebedee, and John his brother;

3 Philip, and Bartholomew; Thomas, and Matthew the publican; James the son of Alphaeus, and Lebbaeus, whose surname was Thaddaeus;

4 Simon the Canaanite, and Judas Iscariot, who also betrayed him.

5 ¶ These twelve Jesus sent forth, and commanded them, saying, go not into the way of the Gentiles, and into any city of the Samaritans enter ye not:

6 But go rather to the lost sheep of the house of Israel.

7 And as ye go, preach, saying, the kingdom of heaven is at hand.

8 Heal the sick, cleanse the lepers, raise the dead, cast out devils: freely ye have received, freely give.

Luke 9:1-6

1 ¶ Then He called His twelve disciples together and gave them power and authority over all demons, and to cure diseases.

2 He sent them to preach the kingdom of God and to heal the sick.

3 And He said to them, "Take nothing for the journey, neither staffs nor bag nor bread nor money; and do not have two tunics apiece.

4 "Whatever house you enter, stay there, and from there depart.

5 "And whoever will not receive you, when you go out of that city, shake off the very dust from your feet as a testimony against them."

6 So they departed and went through the towns, preaching the gospel and healing everywhere.

I deliberately gave the above Scriptures for you to see the importance of The Word of God as His Agency that sets the stage for His healing to be manifested.

Every Shepherd, therefore, MUST feed the sheep or flock with God's wisdom and knowledge if they are to be free from lack and want.

Jeremiah 23:1-4

1 ¶ Woe be unto the pastors that destroy and scatter the sheep of my pasture! saith the LORD.

2 Therefore thus saith the LORD God of Israel against the pastors that feed my people; Ye have scattered my flock, and driven them away, and have not visited them: behold, I will visit upon you the evil of your doings, saith the LORD.

3 And I will gather the remnant of my flock out of all countries whither I have driven them, and will bring them again to their folds; and they shall be fruitful and increase.

4 And I will set up shepherds over them which shall feed them: and they shall fear no more, nor be dismayed, neither shall they be lacking, saith the LORD.

Jeremiah 3:15-16

15 And I will give you pastors according to mine heart, which shall feed you with knowledge and understanding.

16 And it shall come to pass, when ye be multiplied and increased in the land, in those days, saith the LORD, they shall say no more, The ark of the covenant of the LORD: neither shall it come to mind: neither shall they remember it; neither shall they visit it; neither shall that be done any more.

Jesus Christ was a relevant Shepherd to the sheep and flock of God.

Your story and testimony will not be different from His.
So, shall it be in Jesus Name.
I am expecting your testimonies.

BECOME A CITIZEN OF HEAVEN TODAY!

Please note, if you are not yet a Citizen of Heaven, but desire to be, this is your opportunity. To be a citizen of Heaven, you must be from above. You must be born of God. You must be born again!

John 3:3-8,12-13

3 Jesus answered and said to him, "Most assuredly, I say to you, unless one is born again, he cannot see the kingdom of God."

4 Nicodemus said to Him, "How can a man be born when he is old? Can he enter a second time into his mother's womb and be born?"

5 Jesus answered, "Most assuredly, I say to you, unless one is born of water and the Spirit, he cannot enter the kingdom of God.

6 "That which is born of the flesh is flesh, and that which is born of the Spirit is spirit.

7 "Do not marvel that I said to you, 'You must be born again.'

8 "The wind blows where it wishes, and you hear the sound of it, but cannot tell where it comes from and where it goes. So is everyone who is born of the Spirit."

12 If I have told you earthly things, and ye believe not, how shall ye believe, if I tell you of heavenly things?

13 And no man hath ascended up to heaven, but he that came down from heaven, even the Son of man which is in heaven.

Jesus says "You must be born again to live and enjoy Heaven-now!" John 3:3,7

No matter your sin(s) and what you may have done, God wants you forgive and restored now!

John 3:13-18

13 "No one has ascended to heaven but He who came down from heaven, that is, the Son of Man who is in heaven.

14 "And as Moses lifted up the serpent in the wilderness, even so must the Son of Man be lifted up,

15 "that whoever believes in Him should not perish but have eternal life.

16 "For God so loved the world that He gave His only begotten Son, that whoever believes in Him should not perish but have everlasting life.

17 "For God did not send His Son into the world to condemn the world, but that the world through Him might be saved.

18 "He who believes in Him is not condemned; but he who does not believe is condemned already, because he has not believed in the name of the only begotten Son of God.

Remember God gives the power to become His son to everyone that receives Jesus as The Christ, The Son of The Living God or believe in His Name. John 1:12

Remember God Himself dwells in everyone who believes and confesses that Jesus is The Christ, The Son of The Living God. 1John 5:1, 4-5;1John 4:4,15

Remember God did not send His Son into the world to condemn the world but that through Him, the world might be saved. John 3:17

Beloved, AS the Father sent Jesus The Christ, even so has The Lord Jesus Christ sent me so that everyone who will believe and receive me as His Ambassador will be saved, healed, delivered and restored. The Lord said to me: As the Father sent Me, even so have I sent you! John 17:18; John 20:21

The Lord said to Me: Verily, verily I say to you, whoever receives you receives me, and whoever receives me receives the Father who sent me. John 13:20.

The Lord said to Me: Whoever rejects you rejects me, and whoever rejects Me rejects The Father who sent Me. Luke 10:16

The Lord said to Me: Behold I give unto you power to tread upon serpents and scorpions and over all the power of the enemy and nothing shall by any means hurt you. Luke 10:19

The Lord said to Me: Behold, I send in the midst of many peoples, like dew from the LORD, like showers on the grass, that tarry for no man nor wait for the sons of men. Behold, you shall be among the Gentiles, In the midst of many peoples, like a lion among the beasts of the forest, like a young lion among flocks of sheep, Who, if he passes through, both treads down and tears in pieces, and none can deliver. Your hand shall be lifted against your adversaries, and all your enemies shall be cut off. Micah 5:7-9

The Lord said to Me: You will be like the dew to all My people and creation; You shall grow like the lily, and lengthen Your roots like Lebanon. Your branches shall spread; Your beauty shall be like an olive tree, And Your fragrance like Lebanon. Those who dwell under Your shadow shall return; They shall be revived like grain, and grow like a vine. Their scent shall be like the wine of Lebanon. Hosea 14:5-7

Beloved, there is no justifiable reason under Heaven why you should ever go through ANYTHING that is not in Heaven now!

Beloved there is no justifiable reason why you should not have NOW the best God has fully paid for and credited to your personal account!

Hear Me: All things are ready. And all things are yours! What are you still waiting for? All you need to do is to believe that Jesus is the Christ, The Son of The Living God. And He sent Me to bring this Goodnews to you.

Your struggles can come to an end today. You can be enrolled into Heaven's citizenship right now. You can begin a new life today and enjoy all that is available in Heaven from this day forward. The Lord Jesus Christ who sent me confirms with undeniable proof that He is ALIVE today in the lives of those who hear my words and believes in Him [The Lord Jesus Christ] who sent me.

Jesus is alive today and the only way to prove it is for Him to do what He did before in your life today. He sent me and will prove to you that this is not a made-up story written to impress you, but His ordained will made available to make you are created to be!

The choice is yours! Rise and take what belong to you and enter your rest!

Peace now and always in Jesus Almighty Name!

Amen!!!

If You are not certain that You are Born Again as you are certain of your name, or You were once saved but went astray again, living and doing as you pleased, then say this Prayer aloud now for you to become a citizen of Heaven:

PRAYER FOR SALVATION AND RESTORATION TO HEAVEN'S CITIZENSHIP!

Dear Heavenly Father, I return to you by Faith. I am sorry for my sins. I believe in my heart that Jesus is The Christ and that He died for my sins and rose from the dead on the third day, according to Scripture, for my justification. I confess that Jesus Christ is LORD and I accept Him now as my Saviour. I believe my sins are wiped away.

I call upon The Name of The LORD for my total Healing, Liberty and Restoration.

I ask for the Gift of Your Holy Spirit, Power and Grace to follow and serve You from this day forward. And I Thank You Abba Father for doing far beyond all I have asked and can ever imagine in Jesus Name. Amen!

I Now Declare That I Am A Child of God Forever! There's no going back.

Now that you have become a Citizen of Heaven, you need to upgrade by signing up to serve as an Ambassador for Christ. That is where your security and relevance lie. There is no job in this world that can be compared to serving as The Ambassador of The King of kings and Lord of lords. The benefits are amazing. You cannot do a better or more honourable job.

You can Enlist now and become a Partner or a Member of

our Totally Empowered Ambassadors on Mission (TEAM) and see what Our Risen Lord and King Jesus Christ will transform your life into and do in, for and through you from this day as you believe and obey His Word!

I can't wait to hear from you because I believe you have been blessed and helped immensely reading this Book as much as I am writing it! I am praying for you.

ABOUT THE AUTHOR

Amb. Promise Ogbonna

Amb Promise Ogbonna is the President of Christ's Ambassadors Living Mission International Inc. aka Jesus Mission Headquarters, an all-encompassing network of ministries with a mandate focus to Preach The Everlasting Gospel to all, Stop anything after man's destruction, Bring Healing, Liberty and Restoration to all, Make ALL Christ's Ambassadors and Make Heaven-Now a Reality for All.

He is the Publisher of ONTOP Life Publishers Company with a commission to Publish the Everlasting Gospel and Bring God's Wisdom-solutions for every problem and need of mankind.

He represents The Lord Jesus Christ and serves Him as His Ambassador!

He is married and blessed with children.

OTHER BOOKS BY AMB PROMISE OGBONNA

1. The Nothingness of Satan
2. You Can Make a Fresh Start and Rule Your World
3. Restoring the Forgotten Dignity of Woman
4. Christ's Ambassadors: Re-Emergence of Rulers in
5. Why Prophet Elisha Died Sick and how to Avoid it
6. You Can Choose When to Die
7. You Shall Live and Not Die
8. Why Christians Die Sick
9. 7 Keys to Undeniable Healing
10. 8 Decisive Hours That Will Take You to The Topmost
11. Activating God's Medicine for Your Healing
12. God Cannot Fail to Heal You
13. Healing Is Your Legal Right
14. God's Final Solution to The Problem of The Black Race
15. Understanding God's Secret to Winning Life's Battles
16. 100 Years Is Minimum
17. How to Raise the Dead
18. Manifesting as Signs and Wonders: Unlocking the Unstoppable You Regardless of Where You are Now!
19. 40 Pitfalls to Avoid in Life – Mastering the Art of Living Successfully.
20. Wisdom Seeds to Greatness in Life – Inspiring Seed-Thoughts on Being Your Best
21. God's Medicine for Incurable Diseases
22. Ambassador Promise: Jesus Christ's Official Ambassador and T. L. Osborn's Successor on Earth Today! Appearance and En-

counters with The Lord Jesus Christ, Mantles of Notable Servants of God Received and the 9 Mandates.

23. Simple Faith for Supernatural Success
24. God's Final Message to The Poor
25. Understanding the Gospel to The Poor
26. Faith That Attracts God's Attention and Results
27. God's Quickest Way to Your Prosperity and Restoration
28. Faith for Healing
29. Unveiling God's Master Keys to Your Dominion Against All Odds
30. Operating the Faith that Pleases God
31. 4 Kinds of People the Lord Will Heal
32. Appropriating Your Healing
33. Why Divine Healing
34. Secrets to Making Your Faith Work
35. The Right Use of The Anointing Oil
36. Healing All Manner of Sicknesses & Diseases
37. Christ's Ambassadors Handbook: Volume 1
38. Christ's Ambassadors Handbook: Volume 2
39. Christ's Ambassadors Handbook: Volume 3
40. God's Secret to Wealth and Health
41. Enforcing Your Covenant of Divine Health
42. Faith for Miracles
43. Christ's Teaching on God's Secret to Kingdom Prosperity
44. The Prerequisite for Doing God's Will and Finishing His Work
45. The Wonders of The New Creation
46. Secrets to Being A Relevant Shepherd & Minister of Christ

UPCOMING BOOKS BY AMB PROMISE OGBONNA

1. Enforcing Kingdom Wealth Transfer
2. God's Final Word on Tithes, Tithing and Offerings
3. Creating Heaven Out of Your Ruined World
4. How to Attract God's Blessing on Your Business and Career
5. God's Master Key to Your Dominion
6. Wisdom Keys to God's Recovery Plan
7. Why People Fail in Life –Secrets to Success without Stress

Please visit your favorite eBook retailer to discover other books by Amb Promise Ogbonna.

CONNECT WITH AMB PROMISE OGBONNA

I appreciate you reading my book. Here are my links and Social Coordinates

Send Amb Promise Ogbonna a mail at:

Visit Amb. Promise Ogbonna's Website:

Subscribe to Amb Promise Ogbonna's videos at:

Follow Amb Promise Ogbonna on Twitter:

Friend Amb Promise Ogbonna on Facebook:

Connect with Amb Promise Ogbonna on LinkedIn:

Read Amb Promise Ogbonna's Story at Wattpad:

Subscribe to Amb Promise Ogbonna's Blog at:

Follow Amb Promise Ogbonna on Instagram:

Subscribe to Amb. Promise Ogbonna's HEAVENow You Tube Channel:

Read Amb Promise Ogbonna's Smashwords Interview at

Read Amb Promise Ogbonna's Author Profile at Smashwords:

Follow Amb Promise Ogbonna at Amazon:

Connect with Amb Promise Ogbonna on Pinterest:

Read Amb. Promise Ogbonna books at Okada Books:

Get Access to all the Books of Amb Promise Ogbonna at Books2Read Universal Book Link:

Join Amb. Promise Ogbonna in HEAVENow Services

Worship with Ambassador Promise in Christ's Ambassadors Heaven-Now Services at:

Christ's Ambassadors Living Mission International [Jesus Mission Headquarters]

24 Independence Street, Behind O'Mark Schools by O'Mark Bus Stop, LASU Road, Igando Lagos

Wednesdays: 12:00-1:00pm. Hour of EmPowerment for All [Online]

Saturdays: 8:00-9:00am. Hour of Healing for All

Sundays: 8:00-9:00am. Hour of Liberty and Restoration for All

Sundays: 9:00-10:00am. Hour of Kingdom Wealth Transfer for All

Last Friday Night Monthly: 10pm. Night of Restorations for All

Ambassadors International Bible Institute: Runs Online and Offline Courses to Make Christ's Ambassadors and Make Heaven Now a reality for all. Enroll today!

HEAVENow...Making Heaven now a Reality for ALL!

OUR HEALING PRODUCTS

We are on a Mission to Bring Healing to the sick no matter their sicknesses or diseases and Restore Health, Wealth and Peace to ALL! Here are some of our Products and Services we run to Bring Healing to the sick worldwide!

1. All-Purpose Divine Healing Medicine
2. Healing Messages – Podcasts, CD, MP3 and DVD
3. Healing Books
4. Healing Leaves Magazine
5. Healing Anointing Oil
6. Healing Mantles and Clothes
7. Healing Materials
8. Healing Elixir for incurable diseases
9. Healing Songs
10. Healing Homes
11. Health Centers
12. Healing Balm

Call us today for all of your Healing needs! We are here to SERVE YOU!

For Bookings Contact Amb Promise Ogbonna at: ambpromiseogbonna@gmail.com or Call +234 8060638053

OUR SPECIAL SERVICES

We Offer the following services to Churches, Ministries, Corporate Bodies, Businesses, Communities, Groups, International Bodies, NGO's, Governments, States and Nations.

1. Healing Seminars
2. Healing School
3. Healing Teams
4. Healing Outreaches and Explosions
5. World Healing Conferences
6. Health and Wealth Trainings
7. Heaven-Now Campaigns
8. Kingdom Wealth Transfer Seminars
9. God's FASTEST Prosperity Recovery Seminars
10. Heaven's Business School
11. Time and Stress Management Training
12. Leadership Responsibility Development Training

Our Services are geared towards making every person fit spirit, soul and body so that they can be empowered to deliver results competently, effectively and efficiently.

For Bookings Contact Amb Promise Ogbonna at: ambpromiseogbonna@gmail.com or Call +234 8060638053